ICSC's
GUIDE TO
SHOPPING
CENTER
TERMS

ICSC's
GUIDE TO
SHOPPING
CENTER
TERMS

International Council of Shopping Centers
NEW YORK

About the International Council of Shopping Centers

The International Council of Shopping Centers (ICSC) is the trade association of the shopping center industry. Serving the shopping center industry since 1957, ICSC is a not-for-profit organization with more than 27,000 members in 58 countries worldwide.

ICSC members include shopping center

- owners
- developers
- managers
- marketing specialists
- leasing agents
- retailers
- researchers
- architects
- contractors
- consultants
- investors
- lenders and brokers
- academics
- public officials.

ICSC sponsors approximately 300 meetings a year and provides a wide array of services and products for shopping center professionals, including publications and research data.

For more information about ICSC, write or call:
International Council of Shopping Centers
665 Fifth Avenue
New York, NY 10022-5370
Telephone: (212) 421-8181
Fax: (212) 486-0849

Published by
INTERNATIONAL COUNCIL OF SHOPPING CENTERS
Publications Department
665 Fifth Avenue
New York, NY 10022-5370

Text design: Stanley S. Drate/Folio Graphics Company, Inc.
Cover design: The Great American Art Company
ICSC Catalog Number: 093

International Standard Book Number: 0-927547-48-1

Printed in the United States of America

CONTENTS

ABOUT THIS BOOK   *vii*

ICSC SOURCES OF
SHOPPING CENTER TERMS   *ix*

SHOPPING CENTER TERMS   *1*

ADDITIONAL SOURCES OF TERMS   *145*

ABOUT THIS BOOK

ICSC's Guide to Shopping Center Terms brings together in one book hundreds of definitions of shopping center terms compiled solely from ICSC publications that cover the following industry disciplines:

- Management
- Marketing
- Design and construction
- Leasing
- Retailing.

Financial, roofing, parking lot, insurance, and other terms are also included, among others.

This book has been compiled for use by anyone who needs a definition of a shopping center term. The guide will assist newcomers in learning the jargon of the industry. Seasoned professionals can refer to this guide to find definitions of new industry terms, to get further explanations or clarification of a term they are not clear on, or to understand the language used by a shopping center colleague in a shopping center discipline other than their own.

The glossary that follows lists key terms and definitions. The terms are defined within the context of the shopping center subject area in which they originally appeared.

Except for the occasional word that has been added to clarify a term that needed explanation after being taken out of the context of its original subject area, no attempt has been made to re-write or resolve differences in the terms and definitions. The added words appear in square brackets.

Each term has a numerical footnote accompanying it to indicate the source from which it is reprinted. Readers can thus understand the context in which the term was originally used and can access the definition's original source for further information if desired.

When one term is defined in several books, all the definitions are included as a multiple definition listing.

ICSC SOURCES
OF
SHOPPING CENTER TERMS

A list of the ICSC publications from which the terms in this book were taken is given below. The number preceding each title corresponds to the footnote number shown in the definitions.

1. *ICSC Research Quarterly,* "Shopping Center Definitions."
2. *Marketing Your Shopping Center,* S. Albert Wenner.
3. *Fundamentals of Shopping Center Management.*
   "Center Recordkeeping and Accounting"
   "The Fundamentals of Retailing"
   "Marketing: An Overview"
   "Maintaining Your Center"
   "Security and Safety"
   "Understanding Leases"
4. *ICSC Keys to Shopping Center Marketing Series.*
   "Administration"
   "Advertising"
   "Marketing Research"

"Media Mix and Planning"
"Overview"
"Public Relations"
"Retailing"
"Tenant Mix and Merchandising"
5. *Fundamentals of Shopping Center Marketing.*
   "Advertising and Effective Use of Media"
   "Basic Budgeting"
   "Market Research"
   "The Marketing Plan"
   "Retailing for Marketing Directors"
   "Working With Tenants"
6. *Market Research for Shopping Centers,* edited by Ruben A. Roca.
7. *ICSC Keys to Shopping Center Management Series.*
   "Financial Concepts"
   "Insurance and Risk Management"
   "The Lease and Its Language"
   "Leasing Strategies"
   "Maintenance"
   "Management Overview"
   "Marketing"
   "Retailing"
   "The Security Process"
8. *Preparing a Budget for a Small Shopping Center,* Alan A. Alexander, CSM.
9. *Shopping Center Lease Administration,* Alan A. Alexander, CSM.
10. *The SCORE: ICSC's Handbook on Shopping Center Operations, Revenues & Expenses, 1993.*
11. *Construction Management Techniques,* Ray G. Simms.

12. *Carpenter's Shopping Center Management,* edited by Robert J. Flynn, CSM.
13. *Advanced Shopping Center Management: Roofs.*
14. *Advanced Shopping Center Management: Parking Lots.*

ICSC's
GUIDE TO
SHOPPING
CENTER
TERMS

ABC Report Audit Bureau of Circulations Report. An audited report of newspaper circulation researched and published by this independent firm.[4]

abstract A summary. A shortened version outlining the main points of a document.[3]

access time The half hour in prime time [television] (7:30–8:00 P.M. Eastern Standard Time Monday–Saturday) that the networks have been required to turn back to the local stations. Network-originated programming in prime time is only three hours per night Monday through Saturday, four hours on Sunday.[5]

account executive One who supervises client use of print and electronic media as advertising agency representative.[2]

accounts receivable All income that has been billed and is still owed at any point in time.[4]

accrual basis of accounting
The method of accounting whereby revenues and expenses are identified with specific periods of time, such as a month or year, and are recorded

as incurred, along with acquired assets, without regard to the date of receipt or payment of cash; distinguished from cash basis.[3]

An accounting method that tracks expenditures against the budget for a given time frame, indicating amounts already received and paid as well as anticipated receipts and planned expenditures.[4]

ad grid   A system of presenting rates that assigns various values to each time period. Broadcast time can be offered and sold in terms of grids.[2]

add-on [rent charges]   Additional charges to the rent, which may include service charges for maintenance of common areas, merchants' association fees, contribution to the marketing fund, HVAC [heating, ventilation and air-conditioning] and electric charges, trash, insurance, or taxes.[4]

ADI   *See* area of dominant influence.

adjacency
On a [television or radio] station, the period of time immediately following or preceding a regularly scheduled program. Also used almost interchangeably with "spot," thus "the Dallas adjacency at 9:00 P.M."[5]

A program or time period that immediately precedes or follows a scheduled program on radio or television.[2]

administrative marketing costs   The cost of payroll, benefits, rent, and bookkeeping and other administrative costs attributed to marketing.[10]

advance   A story, feature or copy of a speech distributed to the media before the event takes place.[4]

advertising   The nonpersonal communication of a sales message to actual or potential purchasers by a person or organization selling a product or service, delivered through a paid medium for the purpose of influencing the buying behavior of those purchasers.[3]

advertising campaign   Advertising and related efforts used on behalf of a shopping center in the attainment of predetermined goals.[2]

advertising fund   A fund set up by the [shopping center] developer for producing special ad campaigns or catalogs for the shopping center.[4]

advertising plan   A description of the message, themes, and creative elements of your advertising campaign. It includes a budget for creative and production services.[4]

agate lines   A newspaper advertising unit of measurement. An agate line is one column wide by one-fourteenth inch deep.[2]

aggregate   Gravel, crushed stone, slag or marble embedded in a flood coat of hot bitumen as the top surface for built-up roofs.[13]

aided recall   A research technique that uses prompting questions or materials to aid a respondent's memory of the original exposure situation.[2]

air check   A tape of an actual [television or radio] broadcast that serves as file copy and which the sponsor may use to evaluate the content.[2]

alligatoring [Also known as alligator cracks]
Shrinkage cracking of the bituminous surface of a built-up roof, producing a pattern resembling an alligator's hide. It results from solar radiation and exposure to the elements.[3]

alteration costs Costs incurred in altering and finishing merchandise to meet the needs of customers at the time of sale.[4]

anchor store
A major store (usually a chain store) in a shopping center having substantial economic strength and occupying a large square footage.[3]

A major department store branch in a shopping center.[2]

The stores and other uses that occupy the largest spaces in a center and serve as the primary traffic generators. Freestanding anchors are excluded.[10]

angle The emphasis or slant of a story.[4]

answer print A composite print of sound, music, and opticals leading to a master print from which duplicates are made for distribution.[2]

approach (outdoor) The distance measured along the line traveled from the point where [an advertising] poster becomes visible to a point where the copy ceases to be readable.[2]

arbitron
American Research Bureau (ARB). The company which produces local spot television and

radio audience reports. All spot television and radio buys should be made using ARB audience figures.[5]

A device for recording when the television is on; a part of a research operation.[2]

area of dominant influence (ADI)
A group of counties in which the majority of the households watch television stations broadcasting from a particular transmitter city. The U.S. is divided into 208 mutually exclusive ADIs. No county can be in more than one ADI.[5]

A geographic area designated by the Arbitron Ratings Company, which defines a television or radio market for the purpose of measuring viewing and listening audiences.[4]

asphalt   A highly viscous hydrocarbon derived from residue after distillation of petroleum; used as a waterproofing agent in certain built-up roofs and for other purposes.[13]

assault and battery   An attempt or threat, with force or violence, to do corporal harm to another. Under common law, assault and battery are two [separate] crimes. An assault under the common law definition occurs if there is no actual touching or injury of another or corporal harm, merely an attempt. If there is touching of the other person, or injury or corporal harm, then the act is battery rather than assault.[3]

asset
Any owned physical object (tangible) or right (intangible) having a monetary value.[5]

What the business owns. *See* current assets and
fixed assets.[4]

assignment   The transfer to another party of all
a tenant's interests in a lease for the remainder
of the lease term. It is distinguished from a
sublease, in which some portion of the terms of
the lease remains with the primary tenant.[3]

audience
All those who see some part of the editorial
content of a publication, or listen to or see some
part of a broadcast program, or have the opportunity to read an outdoor, transit, or point-of-
purchase advertising message. Synonymous
with total audience.[5]

People who make up the primary and secondary
market areas.[2]

avails
The abbreviation for "availabilities." Avails list
all [television or radio] programs available for
commercial insertions, ratings for the program
or time period for the market or for a target
audience, cost per insertion, cost per rating
point, and more.[4]

A list of spots with their audiences, which a
[television or radio] station has available for
purchase.[5]

average
See mean, median or mode.[4]

A measure of central tendency used to indicate
the size of the data taken as a whole as compared
with that of particular items.[6]

average household income   Estimated average income (salaried income) per household.[6]

average inventory   An average of the stock on hand at representative dates throughout the year or season.[4]

average quarter-hour persons (AQH)   An estimate of the average number of people in a demographic group listening [to the radio] for at least five minutes during a 15-minute period.[4]

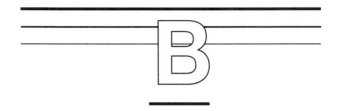

back-to-back Describes the situation where two commercials or programs directly follow each other.[2]

bad debt allowance [Also known as credit loss.] The allowance for uncollectible tenant billing balances.[10]

balance sheet
A statement of financial position of any economic unit disclosing as of a given moment in time its assets, at cost, depreciated cost, or other indicated value; its liabilities; and its ownership equities.[3]

A report showing a business's financial position on a specific date.[7]

See cash flow statement.[4]

bank reconciliation A comparison of the cash disbursements journal with the bank's account record.[4]

banner heading A print media term for a heading positioned across the top of box ad page(s) listing the theme, length of event, and other pertinent details.[2]

banning   A policy by which center security is able to bar a lawbreaker from the shopping center for a finite amount of time.[7]

base sheet   A heavy sheet of felt, asbestos, or organic material, often used as first ply in built-up roofing. Often saturated and factory coated with asphalt. Also used for roof insulation underlayment.[13]

baton   A long, slender but sturdy stick used by center security as a nonlethal weapon. Also known as a billy club or nightstick.[7]

Best Company ratings   The A.M. Best Company quantitatively and qualitatively evaluates the financial condition of insurance carriers. Its ratings reflect company management with an alphabetical rating ranging from A+ down to C. These letters are followed by a financial numerical rating, which reflects the size of the carrier's surplus (equity).[7]

bill-backs   All expense items enumerated in the lease—such as common area, taxes, insurance, and maintenance—that are paid by the landlord and then billed to the tenant.[8]

billboard
1. The common name for an outdoor sign. 2. A radio or television credit naming the sponsor and a slogan, used at the start or close of a program.[2]

1. In outdoor advertising, a term formerly used generally to mean poster. 2. In television advertising, the term refers to special commercial

positions at the start and close of a telecast to announce the name of the sponsor.[5]

birdbath A term used to describe a low area in asphalt paving which tends to collect water.[3]

bitumen
The generic term for a semisolid mixture of hydrocarbons derived from petroleum or coal; used to waterproof roofs. The two basic bitumens used in roofing are asphalt and coal tar pitch.[3]

A hydrocarbon-based substance that is used as the waterproofing element in built-up roofs. Bitumens are either coal-tar based or asphalt-based and are the by-products of the oil-to-gasoline production process.[7]

bleeding [Also known as fat spots.] Sticky black spots that appear on the [parking lot] pavement surface in warm weather. They can be very slippery when wet.[14]

blistering The formation of air- or gas-filled swellings in a roof membrane.[3]

blue line A press proof sheet containing all the elements of an ad, including where color will go.[4]

bodily injury Part of general liability coverage that insures the policyholder against physical injury, including bodily injury, sickness, disease, or death to a third party.[7]

boiler and machinery insurance Coverage for damage caused by or to boilers and machinery, including business interruption caused by boiler explosion or machinery breakdown.[7]

boilerplate   Those clauses of a contract that are generally felt to be typical, standard, prescribed, representative, established, or accepted.[3]

bookkeeping   The process of analyzing, recording, and classifying transactions for the purpose of establishing a basis for recording and reporting the financial affairs of the enterprise and the results of its operations.[3]

box ads   A print media term meaning advertisements, generally uniform in size, grouped together under a banner heading and promoting a cooperative event.[2]

break   The commercial position between two [television or radio] programs. Spots "on the break" are to be distinguished from "in program" commercials. In general, "in program" commercials are thought to have higher recall value than spots "on the break."[5]

breakpoint   In percentage rent, the point at which rent due from a specific percentage of sales equals the minimum rent.[7]

British thermal unit (BTU)   A BTU is the amount of heat required to raise one pound of water one degree Fahrenheit.[7]

broker   A licensed insurance professional who represents and acts on behalf of clients rather than an insurance company.[7]

BTU   *See* British thermal unit.

buckling   Warping or wrinkling of the roof membrane.[13]

budget
An itemized listing and/or allotment of all estimated revenues anticipated and a listing (and segregation) of all estimated costs and expenses that will be incurred in obtaining those revenues over a fixed period of time.[7]

Any financial plan serving as an estimate of and a control over future operations.[5]

A summary of probable income and expenses for a given period of time.[8]

budget billing In this method, the manager distributes copies of the applicable portion of the annual expense budget [to the tenant] and thereafter bills one-twelfth of the total for eleven months, with a final year-end charge adjusted for the by-then-established deficit or surplus.[12]

building code endorsement An addition to property policies that includes coverage for work that might have to be done to comply with building code requirements enacted after the building is constructed.[7]

built-up roof (BUR) A roofing membrane made of alternating layers or plies of felt adhered and made waterproof by the application of asphalt or coal tar bitumens.[7]

bullet loans [Loans on which] only the interest is paid for the term of the loan, with the full principal due upon maturity.[12]

bulk mail A quantity of third-class mail that must be delivered to the post office in bundles presorted by city, state, and ZIP code.[2]

bulk rate contract Reduced advertising rate based upon annual linage used.[2]

bulletin A billboard composed of multiple wooden panels on which a commercial message is painted. Bulletin billboards typically measure 14′ × 48′ or 10′6″ × 36′, with some exceptions.[4]

BUR *See* built-up roof.

burglary Forcible entry into a building [with intent] to commit [a crime].[7]

business interruption insurance Covers loss of net income, other than loss of rents, that would have been earned, including expenses incurred to reduce that loss.[7]

byline The name of an article's writer or reporter, appearing above or at the end of an article.[4]

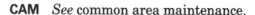

CAM *See* common area maintenance.

CAM administration fee Receipts from tenants for administering CAM [common area maintenance] charges.[10]

camera ready A print media term. A finished, reproducible typeset paste-up of an ad.[2]

cap rate *See* capitalization rate.

capital budget
Includes income from sale of assets, broken down as to gain or loss against book value, payments on the principal of a mortgage or other debt, and the year's outlays for repairs or additions to be capitalized for depreciation over future years. All numbers used in the capital budget are as-estimated going in and as-actual in the year-end report.[12]

An outline of expenditures for physical improvements to the property.[7]

capital costs Money spent on building improvements.[7]

capital expense
A structural repair such as the replacement of a storm sewer system.[7]

The annual amount required to pay interest on and provide for the ultimate return (depreciation or amortization) of the investment.[7]

capitalization   The process of converting into a present value (obtaining the present worth of) a series of anticipated future annual installments of income.[7]

capitalization rate
The rate used to convert income into value.[7]

The capitalization rate varies with the availability of money, the going interest rate in the center's geographical location, the relative amount of risk estimated by a lender, and the overall bargaining position of the developer.[12]

capsheet   The top ply of certain built-up roofs exposed to elements. Usually coated to provide weather resistance.[13]

captive insurer   An insurance company that is sponsored or owned by another entity whose primary purpose is to insure the exposures of its founders.[7]

capture rate analysis   An analysis that assumes retail centers attract expenditure levels relative to their size and location. Thus, a center is more likely to attract a shopper if the center is larger, if it is located nearer the shopper's residence than other centers, or both.[6]

carrier   An insurance company.[7]

cash basis   A basis of keeping accounts (in contrast to the accrual basis) whereby revenue and expenses are recorded on the books of account when received and paid, respectively, without regard to the period to which they apply.[5]

cash disbursement journal   A monthly record of all payments.[4]

cash discount
Percentage off billed price; concession for paying bills within the time period indicated on the invoice. (For example, 2/10 means 2% is deductible from the bill if it is paid within ten days of the invoice date.)[3]

The discount for prompt payment of purchases earned on the goods sold during a specified period.[7]

cash flow analysis   A projection of anticipated income and expenses according to the actual or anticipated times of receipt and disbursement. It indicates a positive or negative cash flow and allows for any necessary adjustments throughout the year.[4]

cash flow statement   A financial picture for a determined period of time. It provides an overview of assets and liabilities, and any variance between them. Also called a balance sheet.[4]

cash method   This report indicates exactly what was received and what was paid to date and relates specifically to the projected cash flow prepared with the budget.[4]

CBD   *See* central business district.

census tracts   Small areas into which large cities and adjacent areas are divided by the Census Bureau. They are designed to be relatively uniform; the average tract has about 4,000 residents.[6]

center mayor   *See* mall mayor.

center-owned   The square footage that is owned by the center and is the leasable area designed for tenant occupancy, including any owned free-standing buildings, plus basements, mezzanines, or upper floors. This does not include the square footage of buildings that are owned by anchor stores.[10]

center rate   The reduced advertising rate arranged between the center and a publication for use by tenants during cooperative centerwide advertised events.[2]

center spread   An advertisement printed across the two facing center pages, including the gutter [inside margin] white space. Outdoors, two adjacent panels using coordinated copy.[2]

central business district (CBD)   Historically, the main shopping or business area of a town or city.[6]

central city   The major city around which Standard Metropolitan Statistical Areas (SMSAs) are defined.[6]

central/urban city center   Located in a major city in one of the U.S. Census Bureau's metropolitan statistical areas, or in a large urban core city in Canada. A center can be located anywhere inside the boundaries of a central/urban city, not just in its downtown area.[10]

centralized [administrative] system   An administrative system in which all financial systems, including payroll, accounts receivable and payable, and purchases originate from a home office rather than from individual shopping centers. *See* decentralized system and hybrid decentralized system.[7]

certificate of insurance
A document that is evidence that an insurance policy has been issued.[7]

A document that verifies the type and amounts of insurance carried by a policyholder.[7]

chart of accounts A systematically arranged list of accounts applicable to a specific concern, giving account names and numbers if any.[5]

Christmas decor/events The cost of seasonal decor and special events during the Christmas season. It includes labor, decorations, signs, point-of-purchase materials, and special entertainment attributable to the Christmas season.[10]

chuckhole *See* pothole.

circular/shopper A preprinted special [advertising] section with a cover paper followed by ads relating to a specific center and event; hand-delivered or inserted into an area publication.[2]

circulation
1. To the Audit Bureau of Circulation this means paid copies of a publication. 2. In broadcast it means the number of [television] set-owning families within range of a station signal. 3. In outdoor advertising, it means the number of people passing an advertisement who have a reasonable chance of seeing it.[5]

The number of copies of a newspaper or circular sold and distributed.[2]

city zone   An area of distribution as defined by the newspaper, typically taking in the city plus surrounding residential areas.[4]

civil liability   The legal responsibility one citizen has to another. It is liability law which applies to an individual who is considered a victim even though no law has been broken. Civil liability is decided in a civil court of law.[7]

claim   A demand to recover payment under an insurance policy; the amount of the loss.[7]

Class A/B/C rates   Rate structure determining rates for the most to the least desirable [advertising] time periods.[2]

close   [In print media] to reach the final stage of preparing to publish, at which [time] no editorial matter or advertisements can be inserted. Also a noun: the close.[4]

cluster shaped [shopping center]   An early form of regional center design. Stores are arranged in a rectangular area, with parking on as many as four sides of the center and with service provided through a tunnel or shielded service bays or a combination of both. Early cluster centers were built as open centers, although some have since been enclosed. The design results in a series of malls. A single-anchor cluster would probably have its anchor store extending from the periphery to the center of the cluster.[12]

clutter   An overabundance of visual and/or audio messages in a given medium.[4]

coal tar
One of two types of bitumen used to construct
built-up roofs.[7]

Bitumen derived from coking of coal. Used as
waterproofing material for minimally sloped
built-up roofs.[13]

COD (cash on delivery) A transaction in which
the customer or buyer agrees to pay when the
goods are received.[3]

coinsurance clause A clause penalizing the insured if the amount insured for is less than a
pre-agreed specified percentage of the value of
the property insured.[7]

color key A proof that indicates both where
color is in an ad and the percentages of color
that will be applied.[4]

column depth/width
A print advertising term. Example: one column
wide by one inch deep.[2]

Depth: The dimension of a column measured
from the top of the page to the bottom, in either
agate lines or inches.[2]

The basic newspaper unit of measurement.[4]

combination rate A single rate charged for insertion in two or more publications, usually
owned by the same publisher.[2]

commencement date The day on which a tenant's lease term begins; not to be confused with
occupancy date.[7]

commercial general liability policy A broad

form of third-party insurance that covers the policyholder in the event of bodily injury, personal injury, and property damage claims.[7]

commercial length   In broadcast, the duration of a commercial, expressed in seconds.[5]

common area
The walkways and areas onto which the stores in a center face and which conduct the flow of customer traffic.[2]

The portions of a shopping center that have been designated and improved for common use by or for the benefit of more than one occupant of the shopping center.[5]

common area HVAC energy   Heating, ventilation, and air-conditioning (HVAC) energy expenses for the common area only.[11]

common area maintenance (CAM)
The amount of money charged to tenants for their shares of maintaining a center's common area.[7]

The charge that a tenant pays for shared services and facilities such as electricity, security, and maintenance of parking lots.[7]

The area maintained in common by all tenants, such as parking lots and common passages. This area is often defined in the lease and may or may not include all physical areas or be paid for by all tenants.[7]

Items charged to common-area maintenance may include cleaning services, parking lot sweeping and maintenance, snow removal, security, and upkeep.[12]

community acceptance Recognition of a shopping center by its market area as an integral part of the community, as well as a purveyor of goods and services.[2]

community center
A community center typically offers a wider range of apparel and other soft goods than the neighborhood center. Among the more common anchors are supermarkets, superdrugstores, and discount department stores. Community center tenants sometimes include off-price retailers selling such items as apparel, home improvement/furnishings, toys, electronics, or sporting goods. The center is usually configured as a strip, in a straight line, or as an "L" or a "U" shape. Of the eight center types, community centers encompass the widest range of formats. For example, certain centers that are anchored by a large discount department store refer to themselves as discount centers. Others with a high percentage of square footage allocated to off-price retailers can be termed off-price centers.[1]

A shopping complex constructed around a junior department store or variety store. Such a center usually lacks a full-line department store. The average size is 150,000 square feet of gross leasable area.[6]

In addition to convenience goods and personal services, [community centers] they typically offer a selection of apparel and home furnishings.

Anchors commonly consist of a junior department store and/or a large variety store in addition to one or more supermarkets. The size
ranges from 100,000 to 300,000 square feet of
GLA and the land area from ten to thirty acres.[12]

community rooms   An area [for public use]
ranging from bare halls equipped with folding
chairs capable of seating perhaps fifty persons,
to quite elaborate facilities accommodating several hundred and providing kitchens, tables,
stages, special lighting, and sound equipment.[12]

compaction   The squeezing of a layer of asphalt
by the addition of another asphalt layer or lift.
Dense asphalt is usually required for parking
lots and roadways.[7]

comparison goods   Merchandise offered by department stores, apparel, furniture, and other
stores in sufficient variety to permit a wide
range of choice and comparison between the
merchandise offered by one store and another.
Comparison-shopping trips are made less often
than shopping trips for convenience items.[6]

competitive effectiveness   That portion of the
total sales capacity of a competitive unit or
group of stores that the unit or group obtains
from *within* the subject trade area. In the prede-
velopment stage, that term refers to the estimated effect existing competitive facilities will
have in the subject trade area after the proposed
shopping center is constructed.[6]

competitive evaluation   An inventory of the
competition and other retail in the market to

pinpoint a center's strengths and weaknesses and determine its competitive position in the market.[4]

competitive facilities   Existing or known future retailing facilities either within or near the trade area that offer merchandise similar to that which will be offered in the proposed center. Note that "low-end" facilities should not be considered in the assessment of competition for higher-quality projects, and vice versa.[6]

compound interest   The interest on interest; interest earned during a given period is added to the principal and included in the next period's interest calculation.[7]

comprehensive   A rough sketch of the idea for an ad.[4]

compressor   The workhorse of an HVAC [heating, ventilation and air-conditioning] unit. The compressor is the hardware that "pushes" hot or cold air out of the system and into the center space.[7]

concession   The privilege of maintaining a subsidiary business within certain premises.[3]

consequential loss coverage   The coverage for consequential loss should include all income derived from tenants. Loss of overage rent is readily computed on the basis of past performance. The loss should be computed on an actual monthly basis rather than treated as one-twelfth of the annual total. Coverage should also include loss of common area maintenance payments and any other tenant charges subject to abatement by lease terms.[12]

consideration Something tangible, usually money, that has been promised or done that binds a legal obligation and makes it enforceable.[7]

constant dollar projections Dollar projections that account for only real growth and not for inflation.[8]

construction allowance Money or financial incentives given to tenants for the cost of constructing their store space in a center.[7]

construction management Construction management is a form of contracting. The construction manager acts as an agent for the developer or owner, taking no risk or financial responsibility for the outcome of the project, which is different from the responsibilities of a general contractor. The construction manager supervises, coordinates, and administers the work on behalf of the developer; however, all contracts are executed directly between the various trade contractors and the developer, with the construction manager signing as an agent of the owner. The construction manager might hire a general contractor or enter into multiple prime contracts with a variety of trade contractors. In either case, if there is a loss or overrun, the dispute is between the developer and the trade contractors, not between the developer and the construction manager.[11]

consumer benchmarks Comparative standards

of shopping patterns and store-related performance.[4]

consumer market research Research based on questionnaire administration of two key types: a random sample survey, generally conducted by telephone within a designated geographic area (the primary trading area of the proposed facility); and an on-site survey of an existing competitive facility.[6]

Consumer Price Index (CPI)
An indicator of rising prices or inflation used to measure the impact of inflation upon consumers; published by the Bureau of Labor Statistics at the end of every month.[6]

Various statistical indexes gathered and published by the federal government as economic indicators.[7]

A monthly government report of prices paid for a standard market basket of goods in various classifications.[4]

contingency plans Procedures to be implemented by security and center staff during an emergency.[7]

continuity An advertising message that runs consistently; used for image-building.[2]

continuous occupancy clause A requirement to fully operate a store during mall hours without interruption or closing.[7]

continuous scheduling A consistent and ongoing presentation of the advertising message designed to reach a given audience repeatedly. For example, a commercial that airs every Thursday and Friday between 6 A.M. and 8 A.M. for 13 weeks.[4]

contract
An agreement by which two legally competent persons promise to obligate each other to do something.[3]

In media usage, a written agreement (usually one year's duration) to use a specified amount of space (print) or air time (radio and TV).[2]

contract security An outside security force hired by the center manager on a contract basis.[7]

contractors
Prior to actual construction, the contractor advises the owner, architect, and engineers on alternative methods of construction, prepares the project's construction budget and master schedule, and provides information and guidance on government approvals, safety requirements, bonding, insurance, local labor agreements, wages, and work rules. During the construction phase, the contractor provides on-site organization and supervision for all elements of the work, provides cost statements and progress billings, and exercises overall financial and administrative control of the project.[11]

Laborers who are hired by center managers for certain tasks. They are called contractors because the work is done according to a written agreement or contract.[7]

convenience goods Goods from drug, grocery, liquor, and hardware stores; services from beauty, barber, and bake shops; and services from laundry and dry cleaning establishments.[6]

convenience shopping center Planned development in which the predominant retailing elements are devoted to providing day-to-day necessities.[6]

cooperative pages Single or facing pages divided into equal-size box ads, headed with a banner giving event details. All ads are in the same typeface; no logos are permitted.[2]

cooperative section *See* circular/shopper or mailer.[2]

copy and layout The visual and copy components of an ad to be typeset by a publication; usually requires a proof.[2]

copy and layout deadline The lead time required to produce an ad and furnish a proof prior to publication.[2]

copy research [Also known as copy testing.] Research to determine the effect of an advertisement or campaign, either before it is disseminated (pretesting) or afterward (post-testing).[5]

core samples A testing process used to determine the condition of roofs or asphalt parking lots and roadways. A core is used to take a vertical sample of the roof or parking lot in question. An expert then surveys the layers to determine if the work was completed as agreed.[7]

cost The price at which goods are purchased in the wholesale market.[7]

cost approach
A method in which the value of a property is derived by estimating the replacement cost of the improvements, deducting the estimated depreciation, and adding the value of the land, as estimated by use of the market-data approach.[7]

The value of a property obtained by estimating the replacement cost of the improvements, deducting the estimated depreciation, and adding the value of the land, as estimated by the use of the market-data approach. A high percentage of appraisals include the cost approach in the analysis, and, in some states, it is obligatory for the assessor to include it in his considerations.[12]

cost per thousand (CPM)
The cost of reaching a thousand people with an ad. The formula is: Total ad cost divided by number of thousands of people reached. For example, if the total cost for a newspaper ad is $500 and the ad is read by 100,000 people, the cost per thousand is five dollars.[4]

Used in comparing media costs. Can mean cost per one thousand readers, viewers, or listeners.[2]

The advertising cost of reaching 1,000 consumers.[4]

The cost of reaching 1,000 individuals in a demographic group. The lower the CPM [cost per thousand], the more efficient the spot. CPM is developed by dividing the cost of a spot by the thousands of homes reached. (*See* efficiency.)[5]

cost-plus contract   A cost-plus contract has no fixed price. Rather, the owner pays the contractor whatever costs are incurred plus a fee for indirect overhead and profit. The fee is either a fixed dollar amount or a percentage of the total project cost.[11]

co-tenancy   A term that refers to a clause inserted into a tenant's lease stipulating that a reduced rent or no rent be paid until an agreed-upon percentage of the center is occupied.[7]

course   Thickness and build-up of composition flashing, consisting of alternate layers of roof cement and felt.[13]

covenant   Words used in a contract whereby the person who is getting or giving something binds himself to the other for the performance (or nonperformance) of a particular act.[3]

cover page   The lead page of a cooperative special [advertising] section that promotes the theme, event day, center hours, and other pertinent information.[2]

coverage
The portion of an area, community, or group that may be reached by an advertising medium.[2]

The extent of the insurance provided by a policy.[7]

CPI [Consumer Price Index] adjustment   An adjustment to the agreed-upon marketing contribution based on changes in the consumer price index.[4]

CPI [Consumer Price Index] rents   Rents that are pegged to rises in the consumer price index.[7]

CPM *See* cost per thousand.

CPM/PCM Cost per thousand per commercial minute.[2]

CPR Cardiopulmonary resuscitation.[7]

credit A bookkeeping entry recording the reduction or elimination of an asset or expense, or the creation of or addition to a liability or item of net worth or revenue.[5]

credit loss *See* bad debt allowance.

cricket A roof slope or swell designed to run rainwater in a certain direction.[7]

criminal liability Liability occurring when a person is harmed by someone who is breaking the law. Redress for criminal liability is argued in a criminal court of law.[7]

cross-promotion A promotion of two different retailers or advertisers whose products are unrelated and noncompetitive.[4]

cross-shopping Purchasing complementary items at different stores or in different departments of a single store.[4]

cume
Abbreviation for cumulative. The unduplicated audience a program or commercial gets if played two or more times in the same environment over a fixed period of time.[2]

The number of unduplicated people and/or homes reached by a given schedule over a given time period.[2]

The number of different persons or households

reached by a number of advertising messages in one media vehicle or a combination of media vehicles over a period of time. Also called net audience or unduplicated audience.[5]

An estimate of the number of different people in a demographic group listening or viewing at least once during a specified time; comparable to a newspaper's circulation.[4]

curb stone A brace system designed to keep HVAC [heating, ventilation and air-conditioning] units from touching a roof.[7]

current asset
Unrestricted cash or other asset held for conversion within a relatively short period into cash or other similar asset, or useful goods or services. Usually the period is one year or less.[5]

Assets that can be converted into cash within 12 months.[7]

current dollar projections Dollar projections that account for both real growth and inflation.[6]

current liability
A short-term debt, regardless of its source, including any liability accrued and deferred and unearned revenue that is to be paid out of current assets or is to be transferred to income within a relatively short period, usually one year or less.[5]

Those things owed and due within 12 months.[7]

customer profile A composite estimate of the

demographic characteristics of the people who buy certain products and the purchase patterns they will produce.[2]

cutline   A photo or illustration caption.[4]

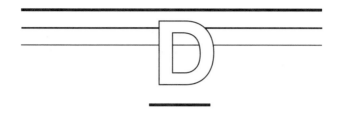

daypart In electronic media, a designated segment of the broadcast day—for example, "Prime."[4]

daytime business population data Demographic and economic information obtained for the worker population of a market area.[4]

DB *See* delayed broadcast.[2]

debit A bookkeeping entry or posting recording the creation of or addition to an asset or expense, or the reduction or elimination of a liability.[5]

debt service The payments consisting of amortization of and interest on a loan.[7]

decentralized [administrative] system An administrative system maintained at individual shopping centers (bookkeeping, accounting, purchasing). Each center is responsible for its work but may follow a standardized system. *See* centralized system and hybrid decentralized system.[7]

declaration The "housekeeping" page on the front of a policy that identifies the policyholder, policy dates, and type and limits of coverage.[7]

deck The base on which roofing insulation is laid.[13]

deductible The portion of first dollar loss assumed by the insured.[7]

default
The failure to perform on an obligation previously committed to. For example, failure to pay rent on a specific date may place a tenant in default of obligations under his lease.[7]

Failure to comply with the terms of a lease.[7]

delamination A built-up roof membrane failure due to separation of felt plies, often resulting in wrinkling and cracking.[13]

delayed broadcast (DB) The airing of a particular program or segment at other than its regularly scheduled broadcast time.[2]

demographic characteristics Basic objective data about the shoppers of a center or residents of a market area. The statistics might include age, gender, income, education, and occupation.[4]

demographic market A demographic group or segment from which a shopping center draws its shoppers and sales.[4]

demographic study A study of socioeconomic facts concerning individuals or households—such as car ownership, income, age, marital status, and education—studied by advertisers and merchandisers in order to make their sales and advertising programs more effective.[5]

demographic multiplier An estimate of average

household size and school-age children for various sizes and configurations of housing.[6]

demographics
Vital statistics of the marketing area; that is, average income, age, number of children, cost of homes, education, and ethnic factors.[2]

Basic objective data about the shoppers in [a geographic] market area. Demographic statistics include age, sex, income, education, and occupation.[7]

The statistical characteristics of population groups, sorted out by such things as age and income, used to identify markets.[7]

DSTM *See* department store type merchandise.

department store type merchandise (DSTM)
DSTM includes the kind of goods sold in shopping centers, such as apparel, shoes, jewelry, gifts and other merchandise usually found in department stores and shopping centers. DSTM excludes personal services, entertainment, food service, drugs, groceries, and automotive, all of which may be found in shopping centers. DSTM sales potential is a component of a center's share of market calculation.[4]

DSTM includes merchandise normally found in variety, apparel, furniture, and appliance stores, and in other outlets such as jewelry, sporting goods, stationery, luggage, and camera stores, as well as department stores.[6]

General merchandise, apparel, furniture, and other merchandise (GAFO) as defined by the

Department of Commerce, *Census of Retail Trade.*[6]

depreciation
The process of estimating and recording lost usefulness. Loosely, any wasting away of a physical asset and hence its cost, especially where not accompanied by a change in outward appearance, as in a slow-moving inventory of styled goods; functional loss of value.[5]

A loss from the upper limit of value caused by deterioration and/or obsolescence.[7]

The amount the value of a property deteriorates in a year; how much the total value is reduced by wear and tear.[7]

designated market area (DMA) A geographic area designed by the A. C. Nielsen Company that defines a television market for the purpose of measuring viewing audiences.[4]

Difference-in-conditions [insurance] A separate insurance package written to cover catastrophic risk.[7]

differential advantage A benefit—feature, location or concept—that will distinguish your shopping center in the mind of the consumer. A differential advantage may be real or perceived.[4]

direct writing company An insurance company whose sales force represents only that one company.[7]

directors and officers liability [insurance] Protects a company's directors and officers in the event of a suit brought by stockholders or the public for negligence in the performance of their responsibilities.[7]

discount-anchored shopping center   A retail development in which a discount store is the major tenant in the development, with additional retail space usually consisting of smaller retail tenants.[6]

discount rate   An interest rate commensurate with perceived risk; used to convert future payments or receipts to present value.[7]

discounted cash flow   The principle of discounted cash flow is that a dollar in hand is of greater value than one to be received at a future time, and the future value progressively diminishes as receipt is further deferred.[12]

display advertising
Newspaper and magazine advertisements designed to attract attention by layout, variety of type, illustration, and relatively large space, and not grouped according to classifications, as in classified advertising.[5]

A print ad bound by a border or an implied border, as opposed to classified or line advertising.[4]

disposable income   That portion of an individual's income after all taxes and Social Security have been deducted; it is the portion which will be invested or spent.[6]

distribution   Area covered by the circulation of a publication.[2]

DMA   *See* designated market area.

documentation   The written or taped recording of the results of an investigation, survey, patrol, or any other activity.[7]

door busters   Small groups of sharply reduced merchandise, with incomplete assortments.[2]

double decker   Outdoor advertising erected one above the other.[2]

double-entry bookkeeping   The method usually followed for recording transactions. It involves formal bookkeeping records, consisting of journals, ledgers, or their equivalent, and supporting documents and files.[5]

double-dumbbell shaped   Essentially a dumbbell-type center. One dumbbell runs longitudinally and a second dumbbell runs latitudinally, forming malls that cross in a central court. This design accommodates four anchor stores and provides parking on four sides of the center and in the intervening U-shaped areas. Service to stores is available through a tunnel or service bays.[12]

double truck   The two centerfold facing pages of ads, including gutter space.[2]

draw tenant   A store that attracts a large volume of customers to the center.[4]

dress code   [A regulation] that defines the type of dress a security officer is to wear while on duty.[7]

drive time
Automobile commuting time, usually 7:00 to 9:00 A.M. and 4:30 to 6:30 P.M.[2]

A radio daypart comprising the hours of 6 A.M. to 10 A.M. and 3 P.M. to 7 P.M. (called morning drive and afternoon drive). These periods are generally characterized by the greatest audience levels of any daypart in terms of total listenership.[5]

dry sheet An unsaturated felt or paper often used on wood decks to prevent asphalt or pitch from penetrating joints. An underlayment.[13]

dumbbell-shaped [shopping center] A double strip of stores placed face-to-face along a mall, with anchor stores placed at both ends of the mall, and with parking on all sides. The dumbbell is designed so that the anchors draw traffic along the mall in an effort to achieve maximum interchange of shoppers.[12]

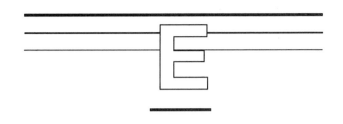

early fringe The time period [in television or radio] usually preceding Prime Time.[2]

economic base The analysis of employment, population, income, retail sales, and other demographic factors that indicate the strengths and weaknesses of a market. Analysis of the economic base aids in determining the need for a regional center.[6]

effective circulation (outdoor) The number of people who have an opportunity to see a billboard: one half of the pedestrians, one quarter of the automobile [riders], and one quarter of the surface public transportation [riders] is considered an effective viewing mix.[2]

effective reach The number of consumers, viewers or listeners exposed to a message enough times (three or more) to be motivated to act on it.[4]

effective rent A combination of the minimum and percentage rent paid by a tenant.[7]

efficiency The cost to reach 1,000 individuals in a demographic group. Generally referred to as CPM, or cost per thousand. To calculate, divide the cost per spot by the audience reached (expressed in thousands).[5]

elasticity factor of spending The increment in spending by a population with higher than average income, but not in direct proportion to income differential; varies from one income group to another and, to some extent, for different retail categories. Generally amounts to 60 percent of income differential for comparison retail. The higher the income, the smaller the elasticity factor (diversion of income to categories other than comparison retail).[6]

emergency book A pamphlet given to new tenants that gives important telephone numbers and outlines procedures for various emergencies.[7]

enclosed common area A term applied to enclosed malls and measured in square feet of floor area. It includes the mall, public restrooms, receiving and distribution facilities for the common use of tenants, and other enclosed common areas.[10]

enclosed mall An enclosed mall has a walkway or mall that is enclosed, heated and cooled, insulated, and lighted. The mall corridor is flanked on one or both sides by storefronts and entrances. The configuration of the center may vary, but on-site parking is usually provided around the perimeter of the center.[10]

end-of-month (EOM) dating Dating that requires the retailer to pay within a certain num-

ber of days from the end of the month during
which the goods were shipped. When a bill is
dated the 26th of the month or later, EOM
dating begins from the end of the following
month.[3]

endorsement   A written addition to a policy.[7]

EOM   End of month.

EOP   End of period.

equity   The net value of a property, obtained by
subtracting from its total value all liens and
other charges against it. The term is frequently
applied to the value of the owner's (as opposed
to the lender's) interest in the property in excess
of all claims and liens.[7]

errors and omissions [insurance] coverage   Protects against liability arising out of errors and
omissions in the performance of professional services.[7]

estoppel letter   The tenant or the landlord represents as to the current relationship of the
tenant and landlord; that is, an estoppel letter
will set forth whether there are any defaults or
whether rent has been paid in advance. This
document would have each party agree that the
lease is in full force and effect and that no
covenant [has been] breached.[7]

excepted property   The basic fire and extended
coverage policy, with rare exceptions, does not
cover boilers and certain other kinds of machinery on which the insurance is written separately
with companies specializing in that field. Also

excluded are trucks, sweepers, and similar mobile equipment, the coverage of which is customarily made part of the casualty insurance. Losses sustained from theft, burglary, and embezzlement are also included in casualty, and all of these things will be spelled out in the excepted-property clause of the fire policy.[12]

excessive force   The use of too much force by a guard during the apprehension or search of a criminal suspect. Determined case by case in a court of law.[7]

exclusion   A provision of [an insurance] policy identifying those things not covered by that policy.[7]

exclusives
A term referring to a store's being given the exclusive right to sell a particular category of merchandise within a shopping center.[7]

An existing tenant may have negotiated the right to be the only one in the center to offer particular goods or services, and therefore space may not be leased to another tenant offering the same goods or services in competition with the first tenant.[7]

exhibits   Attachments, usually to the end of an original lease, specifying the location, legal description, and tenant's construction specifications.[7]

expense recovery   Total receipts from tenants to recover operating expenses for maintenance and repair, utilities, security, insurance, taxes, and other expenses.[10]

expenses Charges involved in running the business. *See* fixed expenses and variable expenses.[7]

expiration date The date on which a tenant's lease term is complete.[7]

export Refers to the export of consumer dollars, usually from an area of limited retail activity to an area of greater retail activity.[6]

exposure That part of the felt [on a built-up roof] covered directly by the bitumen flood coat.[13]

extended coverage [insurance] A fire and extended coverage [insurance] policy routinely includes, in addition to fire, numerous other perils such as windstorm, hail, explosion, riot, and smoke. The same policy customarily also includes the vitally important coverage against what is variously known as consequential loss, use and occupancy, or rental value—the income lost during a restoration period.[12]

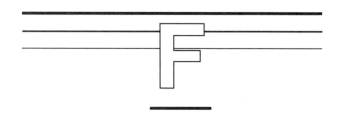

fact sheet Material used to present essential facts about a subject, most often in non-narrative, outline form.[4]

factory outlet A store offering merchandise direct from the manufacturer at prices lower than standard retail. These stores are often contained in centers that specialize in factory outlets.[7]

[fair market] value The price an informed person is willing to pay on the open market.[7]

fall A measurement used for the installation of a drainage system in a parking lot. Fall is the slope or grade from one point, usually to a drain.[7]

fashion/specialty center
A center composed mainly of upscale apparel shops, boutiques and crafts shops carrying selected fashion or unique merchandise of high quality and price. These centers need not be anchored, although sometimes restaurants or entertainment can provide the draw of anchors. The physical design of the center is very sophisticated, emphasizing a rich decor and high-qual-

ity landscaping. These centers usually are found in trade areas having high income levels.[1]

Retail facilities merchandising high-quality merchandise, usually high-priced, primarily apparel and accessories but also including other comparison facilities such as jewelry, luggage, and leather goods; sometimes referred to as high-quality specialty shops.[6]

fat spots   *See* bleeding.

feasibility study   A feasibility study asks the question "Will it work?" Any feasibility study must explore all avenues of approach in determining whether the economic climate is favorable for active and effective implementation of a proposed business or real estate development. The feasibility study is a forecast of things that will most probably occur when the project is "open for business."[5]

feature story   [In the media] a story based on human interest or a particular interest rather than on news.[4]

fee manager   A manager or management firm that contracts to manage a shopping center for a fee or other consideration. A fee manager's relationship with the center's landlord is that of an independent firm hired to render specific services for a specified term of contract.[7]

felony   Generally, an offense for which the sentence provided in the statute is death or imprisonment for one year or more. A crime can also be made a felony by a statement in the statute that the crime defined is felonious.[3]

felt
A fabric manufactured by interlocking fibers mechanically and with moisture and heat. Roofing felts are used to give membranes tensile strength and elasticity. They may be organic or inorganic compounds and are a vital component of built-up roof systems.[3]

A fabric manufactured in a plant that brings fiberglass and binders together. Usually the binders are asphalt.[7]

fidelity bond Employee theft insurance covering monetary loss to the employer caused by a dishonest act of an employee.[7]

fills Materials added to the substrate roof deck to alter its contour; e.g., to achieve slope or to smooth out substrate.[13]

financial reports Monthly statements of how much an account had at the start and the end of the month; they provide both budgeted and actual information for the current month and year to date.[4]

finished mechanical The completed paste-up of an ad in which visual and copy components are ready for reproduction by the print medium.[2]

fire insurance A standard fire policy, often written with an extended coverage endorsement and a vandalism and malicious mischief endorsement.[7]

fixed assets Things used in a business that are not for sale.[4]

fixed contributions [Insertion into] the original

lease of a provision limiting the landlord's contribution in the total real estate burden to a fixed amount—usually expressed as so many cents per square foot of GLA [gross leasable area]—with all taxes over that figure to be spread among the tenants pro rata to their share of the total GLA. The sum to be paid by the landlord is [usually] pegged at approximately the total amount anticipated for the first year.[12]

fixed expenses Also called indirect expenses, these are operating expenses that are not affected by increases or decreases in sales volume.[7]

fixed minimum rent The amount of basic rent paid by the tenant, usually stated as an amount per square foot charged on an annual basis. This figure does not include any other fees or assessments typically charged in a shopping center. Also called base rent.[4]

fixed position spot In television, a commercial which is broadcast at a specified time for the length of the agreement. Often such spots are high-rated and carry a premium price. They differ from announcements in rotating schedules, which only specify placement in broad time periods but do not stipulate exact times for each commercial. In radio, very few stations offer fixed position spots any longer.[5]

flashing Any protective and waterproofing material used to seal the junction of a roof and a vertical wall rising above the roof, or a projection through a roof, such as a chimney, vent pipe, or skylight.[3]

flat rate [In advertising] a uniform charge for space in a medium without regard to the amount of space used or the frequency of insertions.[2]

flat rent A specific rent on square footage paid by a tenant for a specified period of time.[7]

flight [Also known as flighting.]
A series of promotions or events within a single-themed larger promotion to achieve greater impact by utilizing repetition. This is accomplished by enveloping various forms of media.[5]

A scheduling technique in which commercials are scheduled to air for a period of one week or a number of consecutive weeks, then do not air at all for a period of time, after which the schedule is resumed.[4]

flood coat A mopping of bitumen on exposed felts [of a built-up roof] to protect them from weather pending completion of the job.[13]

focus group
A group representing a cross-section of the center's customers, brought together to discuss their needs and preferences.[4]

A group of consumers who are assembled to candidly discuss their opinions on a particular subject.[4]

food court In enclosed malls, an area devoted to permanent vendor stalls offering a range of prepared foods for on-premises consumption and served by a common seating area.[10]

food court expenses All expenses specifically attributable to a food court operation. These include: 1. housekeeping labor—the payroll and employee benefits associated with the janitorial function of the food court, and 2. supplies/other—all costs of supplies and other miscellaneous expenses relating specifically to the food court.[10]

footcandle   A measurement of light. The equivalent of illumination produced by a candle at the distance of one foot.[7]

foreseeability   In the shopping center context, it means that the landlord should be aware that a particular type of crime is likely to occur on shopping center property.[7]

format   The pattern of an advertisement or publication; typeface, size, shape.[2]

FOB   *See* free on board.

free on board (FOB)   A shipping term signifying that the vendor or shipper retains title and pays all charges to an FOB point. For example, FOB New York would indicate that a supplier in New York would not pay freight costs for a purchaser in California.[3]

freestanding stores
Retail stores not located in a planned shopping center or in association with a major business district.[6]

Anchors or nonanchors that are managed as part of the center but are physically separate from the main structure.[10]

frequency
In media exposure, the number of times an individual or household is exposed to a medium

within a given period of time. Frequency of an advertisement is based upon its opportunity for exposure to an audience; in print, the number of times an individual or household is exposed to the same or successive advertisements for the same product in one or different publications; in broadcast, the sum of audiences per telecast in a given time period (four weeks, for instance) divided by the net cumulative audience for that period.[5]

Refers to consistency of advertising; frequent advertising usually results in a rate reduction.[2]

fringe time   The hours directly before and after Prime Time [in television or radio]. May be further specified as early fringe or late fringe.[2]

full position   A special preferred position of an advertisement in a newspaper. Usually refers to an ad placed adjacent to editorial copy.[2]

GAFO An acronym for General merchandise, Apparel, home Furnishings, and Other merchandise (such as books, toys, and food sold away from home), which are normally sold in regional shopping centers.[6]

general and administrative expenses All expenses related to the management of the shopping center, office staff, office supplies, office equipment rental expenses, management fees, leasing fees and commissions, and professional services. [Line items include bad debt allowances, leasing fees and commissions, legal and audit expenses, management fees, office equipment expenses, on-site payroll, and benefits].[10]

GLA *See* gross leasable area.

glossies
Reproducible prints of ads supplied to publications.[12]

Photographs with a shiny—as opposed to matte—finish.[4]

granules Mineral particles of a graded size embedded in the coating asphalt of shingles and roofing.[13]

graphics Descriptive techniques, including sketches, photographs, and all other visual components of an ad.[2]

grease pans Metal reservoirs placed near ventilation units to catch grease before it touches the roof membrane.[7]

grooving Rounded ruts in paving caused by automobile wheels; they may be seen in the main direction of traffic.[3]

gross collectibles The combination of all money transactions handled by the center management on behalf of the tenant. Taxes, minimum rent, percentage rent, and CAM [common area maintenance] fall into this category. This figure is used to determine the management fee of the center.[7]

gross floor area The total floor space of all buildings in a project.[6]

gross income Revenues before deducting any expenses.[5]

gross lease A lease in which the landlord pays 100% of all taxes, insurance, and maintenance associated with the operation of a shopping center.[7]

gross leasable area (GLA)
Normally the total area on which a shopping center tenant pays rent. The GLA includes all selling [space] as well as storage and other miscellaneous space.[6]

The square footage of a shopping center that can generate income by being leased to tenants. This figure does not include the area occupied by department stores or anchor tenants.[4]

The measurement used to define how much space a tenant has leased in a center. GLA is determined by measuring the distance between the middle walls of a space and the distance between front outside wall to back outside wall.[7]

The total floor area designed for tenant occupancy and exclusive use, including basements, mezzanines, and upper floors. It is measured from the center line of joint partitions and from outside wall faces. In short, GLA is that area on which tenants pay rent; it is the area that produces income.[12]

gross margin   The difference between the sales and the total cost of merchandise sold.[7]

gross profit
Net sales less cost of goods sold but before considering selling and general expenses, incidental income, and income deductions.[3]

Markup multiplied by sales price.[7]

gross rating points (GRPs)
The number of rating points a program including commercials has on each area station, multiplied by the number of times it runs within a specified period; example: per week.[2]

The sum of all rating points in the schedule, indicating the estimated reach and frequency of the [media buying schedule].[4]

A rating point is one percent of the total television or radio audience universe. *Gross* rating points are percents (or ratings) expressed on a gross (or duplicated) basis. Since 100% of the homes never have their TV sets turned on at the same time, gross rating points in any quarter hour never add up to 100.[5]

gross sales   Total sales from all transactions.[7]

GRPs   *See* gross rating points.

gutter space   The inside margins of facing printed pages.[2]

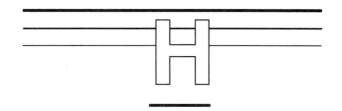

half run In transportation advertising, a car card placed in every other car of the transit system used.[2]

hard goods That class of merchandise, sometimes referred to as hardlines, composed primarily of durable items, such as hardware, machines, heavy appliances, electrical and plumbing fixtures, and farming machinery and supplies.[6]

head The headline or title of an article or story.[4]

head-on position An outdoor poster that directly faces the direction of traffic on a highway.[2]

heat pump A type of HVAC [heating, ventilation and air-conditioning] unit, named for its internal mechanism, which runs on electricity.[7]

heating, ventilation and air-conditioning (HVAC) units Fairly large machines that handle all the heating, cooling, and ventilation uses associated with a center.[7]

hiatus A break in the advertiser's broadcast schedule; a period between flights.[2]

high end   Refers to tenants offering better quality and/or exclusive merchandise at higher prices.[7]

high income per capita   The total income of high-income families and individuals, divided by the total high-income population.[6]

hired car automobile liability [insurance]   [Insurance that] provides contingent coverage for short-term rental vehicles.[7]

hold-harmless agreement   An indemnity agreement in which one party's legal liability for damages is assumed by the other party to the contract. It protects one against losses from someone else's failure to fulfill an obligation.[7]

holdup alarm   An alarm that indicates a holdup is in progress. This type of alarm is usually silent.[7]

house organ   A publication used for communication between management and its employees.[4]

household
Includes all the persons who occupy a group of rooms or a single room that constitutes a housing unit.[6]

The total number of persons, both related and unrelated, residing in a household unit.[6]

housing unit   A house, an apartment, a group of rooms, or a single room occupied or intended for occupancy as separate living quarters.[6]

housekeeping expenses   The cost of janitorial services for the interior common area of the center, whether performed by mall personnel or an outside service. For mall personnel, it includes payroll, employee benefits, and materials and supplies. For outside service contracts, it includes time charges for labor and any charges for equipment use and maintenance supplies.[10]

hut level   The percentage of Homes Using Television during a given time. This number is the sum of the ratings of all stations in a market for the time period.[5]

HVAC   *See* heating, ventilation and air-conditioning.

hybrid decentralized [administrative] system An administrative system that has the characteristics of both decentralized and centralized administrative systems. It takes advantage of computers that tie together such elements as bookkeeping and accounting, but a center manager may do purchasing and approvals, although the center's books are kept at a central location. *See* centralized [administrative] system and decentralized [administrative] system.[7]

image-building A consistent program of advertising and publicity designed to favorably portray a shopping center to the market area in terms of community involvement and the availability of goods and services.[2]

import Consumer dollars from beyond the designated trading area of a retail facility—usually from an area of limited retail activity.[6]

inboard That portion of a trade area lying in the direction of the central city. The effectiveness of a shopping center in attracting patronage from the residents of the inboard side is less than it is for those residents on the opposite, or outboard, direction, since patronage normally flows toward the direction of the central city from the outlying areas.[6]

inch A unit of advertising measurement; a space one inch deep and one column wide. A column inch.[2]

income, net Difference between [the shopping center's] total effective income and total operating expenses.[6]

income, per capita Total personal income of residents divided by the resident population.[6]

income, real The amount of income one can spend on goods and services one may enjoy.[6]

income, total Money "cash" income, including wages, salaries, self-employment, Social Security, and retirement pension.[6]

income, total personal Money income plus non-cash types of income, including food stamps and imputed income.[6]

income approach
An appraisal technique in which the anticipated net income is processed to indicate the capital amount of the investment that produces it. The capital amount, called the capitalized value, is, in effect, the sum of the anticipated annual rents less the loss of interest until the time of collection.[7]

A technique that takes the historical net income as a basis on which to calculate the capital value of the investment producing that net income. According to this method, the value of income-producing property, such as a shopping center, tends to be set by the amount of future income that can reasonably be expected, and the present value of the property is the present value of future income.[12]

income statement A report showing a business's financial performance over a specific period of time.[7]

indemnification Protection against a [law-] suit or [unanticipated] expenses.[7]

indemnity agreement
See hold-harmless agreement.

index   A percent in relation to a norm of 100. For instance, a 123 index means that a number is 23% higher than the norm. An 83 index means that a number is 17% below the norm.[5]

industry averages   Average national sales figures for a given retail category (broken down by year, month, or season).[7]

inflow market   The geographic market located outside the primary and secondary markets from which a center obtains shoppers or sales. Also called tertiary market. *See* primary market and secondary market.[4]

in-house agency   [An advertising agency] installed by owner-developers with a group of shopping centers to create a desired image through the use of the various media; also to provide guidance to the various centers on their budget and promotion programs.[2]

initial assessment   A one-time assessment, equal to one year's dues, charged to new tenants in addition to the standard [merchants' association] annual dues.[4]

initial markup   The first markup placed on an item [offered for sale].[7]

insert   A preprinted section, delivered by insertion in a publication.[2]

insertion order   Written instructions to a publication authorizing insertion of an advertisement and providing specifications.[2]

insolvency   The inability or failure to pay debts as they become due. The condition of an individual or organization in which liabilities exceed the fair and realizable value of the assets available for their settlement.[3]

inspection   A detailed examination of the various physical assets of a shopping center.[7]

institutional advertising   Used to build the reputation of a center or a merchant as the most desirable complex or store in the area offering goods and services to the consumer.[2]

insulation layer   A layer of roofing which lies between the deck and the roof itself.[13]

insurance   A contract between a risk-taker (the insurer) and another party (the insured) in which, for a fee (the premium), the insurer agrees to pay the insured for losses to something specific (the risk) due to named causes (hazards or perils). The insurer may also assume the obligation to pay a third party (the claimant) on behalf of the insured.[7]

insurance expense   This major category includes all premiums and costs incurred for insurance covering structures, public liability, rental value, equipment, and bonding of employees. It includes the cost of an insurance consultant. Line items include: Liability insurance: the net premium cost of public liability insurance; Property insurance: the net premium cost of property insurance; Special coverage: the net premium cost of special coverage, such as earthquake or flood insurance; and Other: the net premium costs of other types of insurance, such as auto, boiler and machinery, bonding of employees, and insurance consultants, if any.[10]

insurance revenue   Receipts from tenants to recover the cost of insurance for the center.[10]

insuring agreement   The section of an insurance policy that states what the policy covers.[7]

integrated commercial   A single broadcast announcement in which the advertiser presents two products using the same announcer and locale. *See* piggyback.[2]

interest   Money paid for the use of capital. It is usually expressed as a rate or percentage of the capital, called the interest rate.[7]

inventory
The goods on hand at a specified accounting date. The term may refer either to the physical goods or to their value.[4]

Physical inventory is determined by actual inspection of the merchandise on hand in the store, stockrooms, and warehouses.[3]

inventory average   An average of the stock on hand at representative dates throughout the year or season.[7]

investigation   The process by which center security officers determine the cause of a crime or accident. This is usually accomplished by interviewing eyewitnesses and documenting their statements.[7]

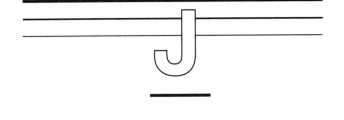

journal The book of original entry in which are recorded transactions not provided for in specialized journals.[5]

junior department store A store that, in both size and selection of merchandise, can be classified as being between a full-line department store and a variety store.[6]

junior unit In print [media], a page size which permits an advertiser to use the same plates for small- and large-page publications.[2]

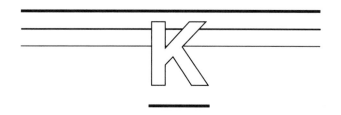

kettle A vessel used to heat bitumen for roof application.[7]

key money Money from the tenant to the landlord for the right to operate a business in the center.[7]

kick-out clause An option that allows a landlord or tenant to terminate the lease before the end of the term. [In the tenant's case, generally tied to the presence of another retailer.][7]

king-size poster An outside transit display placed on the side of a vehicle. Size: 30″ × 144″.[2]

kiosks Booths located in the common areas of the center or mall and generally housing small-item merchandise or services; for example: hosiery, photo developing.[2]

L-shaped [center] A strip center with a line of stores placed at a right angle to it, forming an L, with parking in front of the stores and service lanes behind them. Anchors are usually placed at the ends, but it is possible to place an anchor in the crook formed by the two lines of stores. The L shape is adaptable to corner locations and is used widely for both neighborhood- and community-type centers.[12]

land charges Some leases call for adding to the common area maintenance charge the increases over the base year of the taxes attributable to all of the land within the center, regardless of use.[12]

land use regulations Zoning, ordinances, maps, and subdivision regulations that guide or control land development.[6]

landlord The owner of real property (or of a leasehold interest in real property) who leases the property to a tenant for value consideration.[3]

landscaping expenses The cost of landscaping contracts, services or groundskeepers, and normal replacement of trees, shrubs, and flowers on the exterior and in the interior common area of the mall. It covers the cost of mall personnel, if any, performing these services.[10]

layout   The sketch and design of an ad.[2]

lead   [In print media] the first paragraph of a release or story. It summarizes the most important elements of the story.[4]

leader   A selected item deliberately sold at a price lower than the one at which the largest total profit on the item could be realized in order to attract customers.[4]

lease
A contract transferring the right to the possession and enjoyment of [property] for a definite period of time.[3]

The signed agreement between landlord and tenant that establishes responsibility, sets standards and states what is recoverable from tenants for the maintenance process.[7]

lease summary report   An abstract of information about the status of the leasable space in a center as well as pertinent information from each tenant's lease.[4]

leasing fees and commissions   The expenses incurred for commissions paid to secure tenants for a center.[10]

ledger   A book of accounts; any book of final entry.[5]

legal and audit expenses   The cost of legal services and accounting and audit services.[10]

lessee The tenant; one who rents or leases property from another.[3]

lessor The owner; one who rents or leases property to another.[3]

let To rent or lease.[3]

lethal-weapons policy Guidelines by which security officers are to acquire, use, care for, and be trained in lethal weapons.[7]

letter of intent Generally a document submitted prior to a formal lease. It serves to delineate the intentions between the landlord and the tenant. Basic issues, including minimum rent, percentage rent, pass-through expenses and other major points of negotiation, are outlined. [Generally subject to execution of a complete contract.][7]

letterpress The process of printing directly from an inked, raised surface upon which the paper is impressed.[2]

leverage
The use of borrowed funds to complete an investment transaction. The higher the proportion of borrowed funds used to make the investment, the higher the leverage and the lower the proportion of equity funds.[7]

The level of debt against assets.[7]

liability
An amount owed by one person (a debtor) to another (a creditor).[5]

A legal obligation or responsibility.[7]

Usually a financial obligation and the cost of meeting it.[7]

Those things that can be claimed against the business; what the business owes. *See* current liability and long-term liabilities.[7]

liability insurance *See* commercial general liability policy.

liability limit In the event of a loss, the maximum amount the insurer is required to pay.[7]

lien A charge, security, or encumbrance upon property for the payment of a debt.[3]

lifestyle data A clustering of socioeconomic information based on people who share similar lifestyle characteristics.[4]

lifts The laying of a layer of asphalt on a prepared subgrade or another layer of asphalt.[7]

limited-time station (daytimer) A radio station that is assigned a frequency for broadcasting during specific periods only, sharing its frequency with other stations.[2]

line A unit for measuring space; one fourteenth of a column inch.[2]

line art Illustrative material [other than photographs].[4]

liquidated damages Payments of an agreed-upon amount for the breaching of a contract.[7]

liquidation The sale of assets and the settlement of debts in the winding up of a business, estate, or other economic unit.[3]

liquidity   The ability to convert assets into cash.[7]

list price   The manufacturer's suggested retail price.[7]

local alarm   A detection device that, when activated, sounds a noise alarm.[7]

local [ad] rate
The rate offered to advertisers who do not benefit from coverage beyond their own market area; it is substantially below national rates.[2]

A reduced rate offered by newspapers and broadcast stations to merchants and other local advertisers doing business in the area served by the medium and lower than that offered to national advertisers.[5]

local tenant   A retail tenant who operates one or more stores exclusively in a local market.[7]

logo (logotype) [Also known as sig cut]
The name of a product, service or business rendered in a consistent, distinctive style of lettering, frequently accompanied by a graphic symbol.[4]

A stylized characteristic symbol for sustained identification of a corporation, product, or service.[2]

long-term liabilities   Those things owed after 12 months.[7]

loss   The injury or damage sustained by the insured; in liability policies, it means the payments made by the insurer on behalf of the insured.[7]

loss leader A selected item that is deliberately sold at less than cost in order to attract customers.[7]

low-end [merchandise] Merchandise that has been sharply reduced from original prices, used for sidewalk, moonlight, midnight, and similar limited-period sale events.[2]

lump-sum contracts These contracts are figured from completed plans and specifications by competing contractors who quantify and price the project. Usually submitted by sealed bid, the lowest price is the basis for award of the contract. A lump-sum contract is a "no-peek" contract—in other words, the developer has no right to see what the contractor's actual costs are.[11]

mace A noxious combination of organic chemicals in spray form that is used to disable people. Chemical Mace is a trade name. Mace is illegal in many states.[7]

mailer A preprinted special [advertising] section with a cover page followed by ads relating to a specific center and event, delivered by mail.[2]

maintained markup The difference between the net sales and the gross cost of merchandise sold. It is the margin on sales before making adjustments for cash discounts earned and alteration costs.[7]

maintenance
The upkeep of the various physical assets and common area of a shopping center.[7]

Maintenance involves the preservation of what is already there. For example, patching the parking lot and relamping the lights; painting wall surfaces and replacing deteriorated caulking; rodding the sewer line and changing the oil in the Jeep; and in general doing those things that prolong the economic life of the property in its present form.[12]

maintenance and repair expenses Expenses related to the maintenance and repair of the shopping center. They may include the costs of payroll, employee benefits (taxes, workers' compensation, pension contributions, etc.), service contracts, and maintenance materials and supplies purchased for the center. They usually do not include major capital improvements or maintenance and repair services that are for the benefit of individual tenants and billed directly to the tenants.[10]

major tenant The store that generates the greatest amount of customer patronage to a shopping center. The major tenant, sometimes referred to as the "key tenant" or the "anchor," would be strong enough to stand alone and is effective in attracting patronage from beyond the primary zone of the trade area. Department stores, junior department stores, large variety stores, or supermarkets generally function as major tenants in regional, intermediate, and neighborhood shopping center developments respectively.[6]

makegood
The rerunning of an ad without charge by the medium because of a scheduling or other error committed by it.[2]

A replacement spot (or spots) for a regularly scheduled commercial which was not aired by the station or was aired with a technical problem. Makegoods should always have an audience equal to or larger than the spot being replaced (based on target audience delivery).[5]

mall [The typical mall is] enclosed, with a climate-controlled walkway between two facing rows of stores. The term represents the most common design mode for regional and superregional centers and has become an informal term for these types of centers.[1]

mall manager [The person who] supervises operations and maintenance of center common areas and parking lot, manages personnel, and acts in liaison with the owner/developer, individual tenants, and the marketing director.[2]

mall mayor The merchant who is recognized by peers as an informal leader among the shopping center's tenants. This individual is likely to become the spokesperson for the group.[7]

management fee
The fee charged by the fee manager or the owner to cover rental collection, administration, common area, maintenance, and tenant relations activities.[8]

A tenant and/or landlord charge. The management fee is calculated from a negotiated percentage of the gross collectible of a shopping center. The fee usually includes the CAM [common area maintenance] charge.[7]

The fee, whether a flat fee or a percentage of gross receipts, charged to the center for management services provided by the management company.[10]

mandatory advertising Advertising requirements stipulated in a lease clause. They may include participation in an advertising fund or in center-sponsored cooperative advertising, tenant individual advertising (usually a stated percentage of gross annual sales), documentation of the mandatory advertising expenditures, and tenant reimbursement to the landlord of any shortfall.[4]

markdown
A reduction in the retail price of merchandise, primarily for clearance, special sales events, or to meet competition.[2]

A decrease from the original price of an item. The markdown percentage is usually stated as a percentage of the reduced selling price.[5]

A retail price reduction caused by the inability to sell goods at the original or subsequently determined retail price.[7]

market analysis The process of determining the characteristics of the market and the measurements of its capacity to appeal to a community.[6]

market area The area surrounding a shopping center from which the center draws its customers.[7]

market benchmarks Comparisons of a center's market demographics with other markets in the U.S.[4]

market data The demographic and economic characteristics of a center's market area (based on census data). *See* daytime business population data; lifestyle data; and psychographic data.[4]

market-data approach This appraisal technique, using actual market transactions, is based on the theory that the prices of equal, substitute properties establish value.[12]

market penetration The percentage of the desired market reached by the proposed [advertising] schedule.[4]

market plan
Quite literally, a blueprint for the company's total marketing effort. It charts specific directions, objectives, strategies, and tactics for achieving optimum success in marketing efforts.[3]

A detailed document explaining all the steps and activities a shopping center will use to promote itself during a one-year period.[7]

market profile A demographic description of the people and households of the primary and secondary markets.[2]

market research The initial and ongoing studies needed to make marketing decisions. A survey conducted for the developer before commitment to build and on a recurring basis for the marketing director, who disseminates pertinent information to tenants. Reports define demographics and psychographics of the market area.[2]

market research process The steps followed (in order) when conducting marketing research: 1. Identify information needs; 2. Determine a methodology; 3. Design a research data tool; 4. Collect the data; 5. Analyze the data; 6. Use the findings to make decisions; and 7. Repeat the process.[4]

market sales approach An appraisal technique in which the market value estimate is predicated upon prices paid in actual market transactions and current listings. It is a process of correlation and analysis of similar recently sold properties. Also called the market data or comparable value approach.[7]

market segmentation The designing and implementing of a product or service to meet the needs of a particular group.[2]

market share The portion of trade-area retail potential attributable to proposed facilities, after consideration of their known market strength and relative position vis-à-vis comparable competition.[6]

market study A comprehensive analysis of a center's consumer market. The customers, the demographics, and the competition are all components of a market study.[7]

market value The expected price if a reasonable time is allowed to find a purchaser and if both seller and prospective buyer are fully informed. Market value connotes what a property is actually worth, and market price what it might sell for.[7]

market universe A geographical area of statistical convenience but market representativeness that can be used as the base for statistical computations and derivations.[6]

marketing Everything connected with sales, advertising, sales promotion, public relations and publicity, merchandising, distribution, and research.[5]

marketing director [The person] responsible for all promotion activities, special events, and [maintenance of] budget parameters. Also [responsible for] ongoing market research as a planning tool, community relations, press contacts, and [enforcement of] lease terms relating to tenant participation or violations.[2]

marketing fund
A pool of marketing dollars, to which all tenants contribute, that is administered by the marketing director and an advisory board of tenants.[4]

An alternative to the merchants' association, a marketing fund requires contributions from each tenant; the recipient is not a merchants' association but the fund, which is controlled solely by the developer. Under this arrangement, some sort of advisory board is set up, composed of merchant representatives, and the developer consults with this board on the use of the promotional fund.[5]

The pooling and distribution of money paid by tenants for the overall marketing of the shopping center. The marketing fund is overseen by the center's marketing director and staff and is used for advertising and promotion activities.[7]

Established by a fee paid to the landlord, this is a pool of monies for which shopping center landlords are totally responsible. The fund has a tenant advisory board. A clause in the lease covers increases in the fee.[7]

[marketing fund] advisory board   A group of tenants representing all aspects of the tenant mix that administers a marketing fund along with the marketing director.[4]

markup
The difference between the retail selling price of the merchandise and the cost of the merchandise to the retailer.[7]

The difference between the cost price as billed (before deductions for cash discount) and the retail price at which the merchandise is originally offered.[5]

marriage mail   Two or more messages mailed to a consumer under a single cover or as a package.[4]

masthead   In magazines and newspapers, a listing of the publication's executive and editorial staff and their titles.[4]

mat   Material from which an advertisement is printed.[2]

maximum milline rate   The milline rate of a newspaper computed at its maximum, or highest, rate.[2]

mean
The arithmetic average of a series of numbers, calculated by adding up the numbers in the series and dividing the total by how many numbers there are in the series.[4]

The sum of a collection of measurements divided by the number of measurements.[6]

mechanical   The final paste-up of the type and illustrative components of an ad.[4]

media
In advertising, the means or instruments of communication: radio, television, newspapers, magazines, direct mail, and billboards.[4]

The vehicles—including radio, television, newspapers, magazines and newsletters—through which public relations messages are transmitted.[4]

media alert   A one-page outline of the basic facts of a story. It may also suggest story angles and photos available to illustrate them.[4]

media kit   A packet of information issued to the media that supplies information about a particular event or activity and background information about the sponsoring organization.[4]

media plan   An outline of the media determined to be most efficient for reaching a target market. It defines exactly which media will be used and when. The plan includes the media-buying budget.[4]

media representative   The liaison for center merchants in cooperative promotions; associated with a publication or an electronic medium.[2]

median
The midpoint of a series of numbers. Half of the numbers are greater than the median, and half are less.[4]

The midpoint in a set of numbers, demonstrating there are the same number above and below the midpoint.[6]

membrane   A component of a built-up roof system that is made up of roofing felts laminated with bitumen and top-coated.[3]

merchandise manager   The executive in charge of the merchandise division of a store. In large stores, there are often divisional merchandise managers, each in charge of one of the major merchandise lines.[7]

merchandise mix
The variety and categories of merchandise offered by the retail tenants assembled in a particular shopping center.[7]

A merchandise mix is a group of products that are closely related because they satisfy a class of needs, are used together, or are sold to the same basic market targets. It is made up of a series of demand-related merchandise items, which are specific versions of a product that has a separate designation.[5]

merchandise plan   A forecast, usually by months for a six-month season, of the major elements that enter into gross margin. It normally includes the planning of sales, stocks, purchases, markups, and markdowns.[7]

merchandising   The planning involved in marketing the right merchandise in the right place, at the right time, in the right quantities, and at the right price.[7]

merchants' association
A merchants' association is a not-for-profit corporation organized to conduct merchandising programs, community events, shopping center decoration programs, advertising programs, and publicity programs, and to coordinate joint member cooperative advertising and marketing functions, events, and endeavors for the general benefit of the shopping center. The association acts as a clearinghouse for suggestions, ideas, and programming of merchandising events, and it serves as a quasi-court for handling complaints and differences of opinion.[5]

The tenant group organized to promote the center through cooperative advertising, public relations activity, and community involvement.[2]

An organization of merchants that works to advertise and promote a shopping center. It is a nonprofit, independent corporation.[7]

A not-for-profit, independent corporation with a board of directors who vote and sign checks. The members pay dues. Monthly meetings and an annual report are required.[7]

[merchants' association] articles of incorporation Papers filed with the secretary of the state in which the center is located that declare the [merchants'] association's status as a not-for-profit organization and state the association's purpose.[4]

merchants' association by-laws The basic rules of governance of a merchants' association.[4]

merchants' association dues The financial obligation of member tenants and landlord, fixed by a predetermined structure and used for center-wide promotion, special events, and community activities.[2]

metropolitan area
A geographic area within a market that generally, but not always, corresponds to the U.S. Office of Management and Budget's Statistical Marketing Area (SMA).[4]

A group of whole counties surrounding a major city or twin cities of 50,000 population or more.[6]

metropolitan statistical area (MSA) A geographic unit composed of one or more counties consisting of a population of at least 50,000. Each county must have specific metropolitan characteristics.[4]

midnight sale A centerwide, merchants' association-sponsored, low-end, off-price promotion, generally continuing until 11:00 P.M. or midnight; one night only.[2]

milline rate A unit for measuring newspaper advertising space rates as related to circulation. The formula for determining the rate is line rate × 1 million, divided by total circulation.[2]

minimum rent
The basic rent a tenant pays; usually expressed as a price per square foot.[7]

Rent that is not based on a tenant's sales.[7]

The specific dollar amount paid by a tenant for the amount of square footage leased.[7]

misdemeanor   An offense for which the sentence provided in the statute is less than one year in jail. Any crime which is not a felony is a misdemeanor.[3]

mix   A combination of media, tenants, or merchandise that provides choices for the consumer and balance to the shopping center.[2]

mixed-use centers   These centers typically combine at least three revenue-producing uses from among retail, office, parking, restaurant, hotel, residential, and entertainment facilities. They may be built in suburban or urban areas. In downtown areas, where land costs are high, a multilevel or high-rise, single-mass design is commonly used to minimize the land area needed.[12]

mode   The number most frequently appearing in a set of numbers.[6]

modernization   [This change is] generally considered as having to do with style and appearance rather than utility, such as a new pylon entrance sign or a remodeled building façade.[12]

modified bitumen   A type of built-up roof. Basically, a modified bitumen membrane consists of a combination of roofing felts and bitumen that has been modified by the addition of synthetic rubber or plastic compounds.[7]

mom-and-pop store   A store whose owners own only that single store.[7]

moonlight sale   *See* midnight sale. Hours usually [end] not later than 11:00 P.M.[2]

mortgage constant   The total annual payment of principal and interest (annual debt service) on a level-payment amortized mortgage, expressed as a percentage of the initial principal amount of the loan. It is used in mortgage-equity analysis as well as in estimating cash flows generated by income-producing real estate.[7]

mortgage, wraparound   The owner takes a second mortgage that encompasses the first mortgage. It is a method of refinancing often used when property value has increased significantly and the owner wants to obtain extra funds based on the property's current market value. When a wraparound is used, the borrower avoids losing the benefit of a favorable (lower) interest rate on the original loan even though the new, second mortgage money is borrowed at a higher rate.[12]

motion detector   A device that detects the physical movements of an intruder in a protected area.[7]

MSA   *See* metropolitan statistical area.

multiple percentage rate   A lease agreement in which the percentage rent rate changes at various increments of sales.[7]

multiple prime contracts   In a general contract the developer enters into an agreement with a general contractor who, in turn, enters into subcontracts with trade contractors for masonry, concrete, carpentry, etc. In a multiple prime contract, which is used most often in public works, the owner enters into separate prime contracts with various trade contractors.[11]

mystery shoppers   *See* secret shoppers.

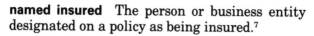

named insured The person or business entity designated on a policy as being insured.[7]

named-peril insurance Coverage that specifies the perils that it covers.[7]

national rate The rate offered to national advertisers (many markets). Used by both print and electronic media, and substantially more costly than a local rate.[2]

national tenant A retailer who operates a chain of stores on a nationwide basis.[7]

natural disaster An emergency created by an act of God.[7]

negligence The act of being extremely careless. The failure to use such care as a reasonably prudent and careful person would use under similar circumstances. If found negligent in a court of law, a center can be held liable for the actions of a guard or a criminal.[7]

negligent hiring Careless hiring on the part of a shopping center that directly or indirectly causes a crime or an accident. If a center is guilty of negligently hiring an employee, it may be held liable for all negative actions by that employee.[7]

negligent retention Retaining the services of an employee despite a poor work record. The center may be held liable for an employee's action if it is determined that the employee should have been terminated prior to an incident or accident.[7]

negligent [security] training The careless training or lack of training of an employee for security work. If it is found in a court of law that a center did not adequately train a security officer who causes an accident or fails to perform adequately, the shopping center may be held liable.[7]

negotiated contract [A contract] arranged on some type of fee basis plus costs with a cap, or guaranteed maximum cost. The fee covers the contractor's indirect (off-site) overhead and profit, while the costs cover all other elements, such as labor, material, subcontracts and job-site supervision.[11]

neighborhood centers
Designed to provide convenience shopping for the day-to-day needs of the immediate neighborhood, these centers are usually anchored by a supermarket supported by stores offering drugs, sundries, snacks, and personal services. The majority of neighborhood centers range from 30,000 to 100,000 square feet of GLA [gross leasable area] and are sited on 3 to 10 acres.[12]

Shopping complexes built around a supermarket as the principal tenant and having a typical gross leasable area of 50,000 square feet.[6]

net   What remains after specified deductions from the gross amount.[7]

net income   *See* income, net.

net operating income   The income after deducting from gross income the operating expenses, including property taxes, insurance, utilities, management fees, heating and cooling expenses, repairs and maintenance, and replacement of equipment.[7]

net price   Sometimes called retailer's cost price. The amount a retailer must pay for a particular item.[7]

net profit
The amount of money left after all expenses have been paid.[4]

The profit over a specified period of a corporation or other business after deducting operating costs and income deductions; equals net income.[5]

net sales   Gross sales less returns and allowances, freight-out, and often cash discounts allowed. In recent years the trend has been to report as net sales the net amount finally received from the customer.[5]

net worth   What the owner actually owns in the business.[7]

news conference   A special meeting to release important information simultaneously to all media.[4]

news release   *See* release.

nonanchors   Stores or establishments that do

not serve as primary traffic generators (generally, tenants), excluding any freestanding units.[10]

noncash expenses   Expenses that are placed in the budget for future billing purposes but are not paid out of the funds held by the manager.[8]

nondisturbance covenant   [A clause in the lease that] usually gives a tenant assurance of continuous operation of its store in the event of the landlord's foreclosure.[7]

nonlethal weapons   Weapons used by center security that, in normal use, cannot kill a human being.[7]

nonpreemptible [spots]   [This refers to] the highest rate charged by a station for a commercial, frequently called a "Section I" rate. In negotiation, spots at lower rates may be classified nonpreemptible as a concession by the station.[8]

nonretail tenants   Shopping center tenants, primarily service-oriented tenants, who do not fit into the traditional category of retailers; a tenant selling services, not goods.[7]

occupancy area The total square footage of a center, including all vacant spaces.[10]

occupancy cost The sum of a tenant's fixed rent, percentage rent, and add-ons. Also called total rent.[4]

occurrence Broadens the definition of "accident" to include incidents that occur over a period of time.[7]

OES *See* optimum effective scheduling.

office equipment expenses The cost of renting or servicing office equipment such as copiers, personal computers, and other office equipment ([sometimes] excluding telephones).[10]

off-price advertising Promotes price-reduced merchandise during a specific sale period.[2]

off-price centers Not to be confused with outlet centers, off-price centers sell branded merchandise that can be found in conventional specialty and department stores at higher prices. Usually the merchandise is first quality. Some manufacturers require that their merchandise be sold without labels in off-price centers.[12]

offset

A reduction in the cost of percentage rent when a tenant meets a prearranged goal in another area, usually sales.[7]

A deduction of specified expenses or investments from all or a portion of percentage rent.[7]

offset printing A process in which an inked impression from a plate is made on a rubber-blanketed cylinder and then transferred to the paper being printed.[2]

on the break *See* break.

one-line budget An abbreviated budget showing only the net balance of probable income less probable expenses.[8]

on-site payroll and benefits All payroll and associated employee benefits related to mall personnel directly involved in the management of the shopping center. This includes the manager, assistant manager, secretary, bookkeeper, and other on-site management staff. This does not include the administrative costs attributable to marketing.[10]

open rate An all-media term. The line, inch, or time cost paid by advertisers without contracts or center rate availability.[2]

open-to-buy

Spendable dollars remaining in the buying plan for a special merchandise category, for a specific period.[2]

The amount of merchandise that may be ordered for delivery during a control period. It is the difference between the planned purchases and the commitments already made for the period.[5]

open windows   Display areas fronting the mall, with no glass enclosure or barriers. Used in enclosed malls only. Fully exposes the store interior to mall passersby.[2]

operating budget
An outline of how much income a shopping center has and how that income will be spent.[7]

Includes all income other than sale of capital assets, offset by all items of expense other than depreciation and interest on debt and payments on debt principal or added investment.[12]

operating expenses
Generally speaking, all expenses, occurring periodically, that are necessary to produce net income before depreciation. Under some conditions these expenses are placed in two categories: operating expenses and fixed charges.[7]

Monies needed to operate a business, as distinct from outlays to finance the business.[7]

operating statement
A management statement that provides net sales, costs, and expenses and net operating profit or loss for a fixed period.[7]

A financial statement showing income and expenses by specific category and for a specific time frame.[8]

optimum effective scheduling (OES)   A scheduling technique, based on a series of mathematical calculations, designed to deliver a minimum of

50% of a radio station's weekly cume an average of 3 or more times.[4]

orbit In television, a type of modified run of station (ROS) schedule, where spots will rotate within a given number of adjacencies, as prime time orbit. Example: Monday, 8:30 P.M.; Tuesday, 9:00 P.M.; Friday, 10:30 P.M. and then repeat.[5]

OTO (one time only) Applies to a spot that is bought to run only once.[5]

outboard That portion of a trade area that lies on the side of a shopping center away from the central city district. The population in this section is normally more effective in patronizing the shopping center than is the population on the inboard side, since its normal traffic movements are oriented in the direction of the central city area.[6]

outlet centers
Usually located in a rural area or occasionally in a tourist location, outlet centers consist mostly of manufacturers' outlet stores selling their own brands at a discount. An outlet center typically is not anchored. A strip configuration is most common, although some are enclosed malls, and others can be arranged in a "village" cluster.[1]

outlot tenant *See* pad tenant.

outparcels Unused portions of a shopping center's site that constitute the perimeter areas, not including the center facility or parking lot, and that may be used or developed for similar or nonsimilar purposes.[7]

overages   Rent paid in addition to an agreed-upon minimum rent.[7]

overhead   A synonym for fixed expenses.[4]

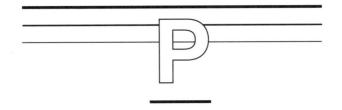

package A group of [television or radio] spots offered for sale together at a given price. A package price is generally lower than the aggregate cost of the spots if bought individually.[5]

pad The exact parcel of land on which a department store's building stands.[12]

pad tenant A tenant, usually freestanding, located on a separate parcel at the front of a shopping center. Also called an out-lot tenant.[8]

paint unit *See* bulletin.[4]

parking area The space in a shopping center devoted to parking, including aisles, walks, islands, minor landscaping, and other features incidental to parking.[6]

parking lot cleaning/sweeping/repair expenses All costs (payroll, benefits, materials, service contracts and supplies) incurred in the striping, repairing of potholes, cleaning, and sweeping of the parking lot, sidewalks and service courts. They also include all expenses incurred in the maintenance and repair of the parking lot sweeping equipment.[10]

parking ratio   The relationship of space used for parking and necessary vehicular and pedestrian movement to land area covered by buildings or space within the buildings. This relationship can be expressed in the number of car spaces per 1,000 square feet of rentable area.[6]

pass-along reader   One who is exposed to a publication that neither he nor any member of his household received by purchase or by request, as in the case of nonpaid publications. Readers from purchase or request households are called primary readers. The total audience of the publication is the sum of primary and pass-along readers.[5]

pass-through expenses   A tenant's portion of expense composed of common area maintenance, taxes and insurance, and any other expenses determined by the landlord to be paid by the tenant.[7]

patching   A procedure used in both roof and asphalt repair. In both cases, it involves repairing a tear, hole, or other type of defect by filling it with an appropriate compound.[7]

pending nonrenewal.   *See* PNR.

penetration ratio   The rate at which stores obtain sales from within a trade area or sector relative to the potential generated. Usually used for existing facilities.[6]

per capita   A means of expressing total municipal expenditures or income by dividing them by the total user or resident population.[6]

per capita income   *See* income, per capita.

per capita retail sales   Total sales for retail categories as defined from a universe such as a metropolitan area, divided by the population of that area and corrected for export/import.[6]

percentage rent
A percentage of the tenant's total annual sales paid in addition to fixed rent. This additional rent is normally paid after a predetermined sales level has been achieved. The percentage factor is then applied to all sales over the present level (breakpoint).[4]

The payment by a tenant as rent of a specified percentage of the gross income from sales made upon the premises. Developers in shopping centers customarily charge a minimum rent plus a percentage rent when sales exceed a certain volume.[5]

Percentage rent is a function of sales activity. A tenant's sales during a lease year are multiplied by the percentage rent rate(s); any excess over the minimum rent is percentage rent.[7]

Extra rent paid to a landlord if a tenant's sales figures exceed a prearranged figure.[7]

perils   Inherent [dangers], such as windstorms or explosions, that can cause a loss or an injury.[7]

perimeter protection   Devices designed to protect the exterior openings of a shopping center—for example, door locks and window bars.[7]

personal injury   A nonstandard part of liability coverage insuring the policyholder, on a named-perils basis, against such things as libel, slander, and unlawful detention.[7]

photo opportunity An occasion for the media to take a photograph.[4]

per inquiry (PI) A method used in direct-response radio and television advertising. Orders are the result of a commercial and go directly to the station; the advertiser pays the station on a per inquiry (or per order) basis.[2]

pica A print media measurement term; one-sixth of an inch, or 6 picas to an inch.[2]

piggyback
The broadcasting of two separate products side by side within the same commercial.[2]

In broadcast, refers to the practice of combining completely separate commercials for two different products (made by the same advertiser) within a single announcement.[5]

pitch To present a story idea to an editor.[4]

plainclothes officers Police officers or security staff allowed to patrol in normal, everyday clothing.[7]

plies The layers of felts and bitumen formed during the creation of a built-up roof.[7]

plot plan The blueprint of a center showing the location and square footage of all tenants, as well as surface facilities.[2]

ply A single layer or thickness of roofing material. Built-up roofs may be three-ply, four-ply, etc., according to the number of layers of felt used to build the membrane.[3]

PNR (pending nonrenewal)   Applies to the purchase of a spot pending the nonrenewal of the contract by the advertiser who already owns that spot (PNR orders are generally used only on the better, higher-rated spots of a station).[5]

point-of-origin survey   A customer survey designed to determine what the primary trading area of a retail facility is by asking customers their home address. These addresses are pinpointed on a street map, allowing the researcher to delineate the trading area of the retail facility. Generally speaking, a minimum sample size of 300 is required to obtain a reasonable degree of accuracy.[6]

point size   The measure of size in which a typeface can be set.[4]

policy   The written insurance contract.[7]

policyholder   The person or company having an insurance contract.[7]

ponding [Also known as ponds.]   *See* birdbath.

poster   An outdoor advertising unit, usually 12′ × 25′, on which a message (printed on paper sheets) is displayed.[4]

posting   The bookkeeping process of transcribing journal entry information to the ledger accounts.[5]

pothole
The commonest type of hole in asphalt pavements. It occurs when a small surface break is

allowed to develop until it involves a larger area; also called chuckhole.[3]

Ever-widening craters that begin as small cracks that are allowed to develop until they involve a large area.[14]

power center   A center dominated by several large anchors, including discount department stores, off-price stores, warehouse clubs, or "category killers," i.e., stores that offer a tremendous selection in a particular merchandise category at low prices. The center typically consists of several freestanding (unconnected) anchors and only a minimum amount of small specialty tenants.[1]

preaudit   A miniaudit professionally conducted 90 days prior to year-end, in advance of a complete annual audit.[4]

preempt   As an electronic media term, time sold at a lower rate and subject to resale by the station if a higher rate is offered.[2]

preemptible spots   Commercial positions sold at lower rates until they can be "recaptured," at the station's discretion, for an advertiser who is willing to pay the full rate. When this occurs, the first advertiser is given the option of paying the higher rate to keep the spot. Preemptible spots are often referred to as "Section II" spots (preemptible on 2 weeks' notice) or "Section III" spots (preemptible immediately). Section III is cheaper than Section II.[5]

preferred positioning   A print media term referring to the desirable positioning of an ad—that is, right-hand pages 3 or 5 or preceding a centerfold.[2]

premium
The amount paid for an insurance policy.[7]

The fee paid to an insurance company as an inducement for assuming part of the insured's risk.[7]

primary market
The geographic market from which a center's predominant shoppers and/or sales come. *See* secondary market.[4]

A geographic term used to define the immediate trading area of a shopping center.[2]

primary research The process of gathering original information because existing data on an issue are not available. *See* secondary research.[4]

primary trading area The geographic area around a particular retail facility from which approximately 60% to 70% of the facility's customers come. The geographic radii and driving times to the primary zone vary among center types.[6]

prime time A television term denoting the hours television viewing is at its peak. Usually 7:30 P.M. to 11:00 P.M., local time, or not less than three continuous hours per broadcast day. The time frame will vary in different locales and with different demographics.[2]

pro rata share The assessment of expenses on a proportional basis between landlord and tenant.[7]

process color In printing, a computer process that layers in colors and blends them at the time of printing.[4]

pro forma The developer's estimate of all costs of planning, developing, building, and operating the center. Then he develops estimates of income, primarily from rents to be paid by tenants. From these estimated expenses and income, the developer computes the anticipated net income for the shopping center. From that item, the projected value of the completed, operating shopping center may be calculated through application of a capitalization rate.[12]

profit A general term for the excess of revenue, proceeds, or selling price over related costs.[5]

profit and loss statement A financial statement showing revenues earned by a business, the expenses incurred in earning the revenues, and the resulting net income or net loss; also called operating statement, variance report, income statement, or statement of income and expenses.[5]

promotion An activity that benefits the center's business purpose. In terms of effect, promotion is intended to directly stimulate shopper traffic and subsequently sales.[12]

promotional license agreement A written agreement between the landlord and an individual or organization staging an event or activity in the shopping center common area that details requirements for insurance, payment, and all other indemnity and limits the landlord's liability resulting from events hosted by outside groups. *See* hold-harmless agreement.[4]

promotions or special events expenses   The cost of producing special events and promotional activities within the center, except at Christmastime. They include labor, decorations, signs, point-of-purchase materials, special entertainments, etc., attributable to such events.[10]

proof
A printed copy of a publication-set ad, submitted to the advertiser for corrections or approval prior to publication.[2]

Copies of an ad for review at different stages in its progress. *See* blue line; color key.[4]

property damage   Part of liability coverage defined as direct damage to physical property and loss of use thereof.[7]

property insurance   First-party insurance covering the insured for damage to his or her personal or real property or the loss of its use.[7]

proprietary security   In-house security developed, managed, and maintained by a center's manager or landlord.[7]

protected premises   A shopping center that has had an alarm system installed.[7]

PruneYard court case   In matters involving political petitions, one landmark decision by the United States Supreme Court, *PruneYard Shopping Center v. Robins*, has had far-reaching effects on shopping centers. Decided in 1980, the PruneYard decision, as it is known, held that the state (California) can require public access to a shopping center for political petitioning under reasonable rules and regulations without violating the shopping center owner's constitutional rights.[12]

PSAs   *See* public service announcements.

psychographics
The motivating forces that influence shopping patterns and consumer behavior.[2]

Information based on categorization of consumer values, motivation, how people are influenced, what they spend their money on, and the psychological attributes they exhibit in terms of shopping behavior.[4]

An interpretation of lifestyle issues: how people are influenced and what they spend their money on.[7]

Factors about lifestyle that influence how and on what people spend their money.[4]

psychological testing An examination performed by a psychologist to determine the emotional stability of a person.[7]

public relations   The establishment and maintenance of goodwill, promulgated by participation and concern for communitywide activities.[2]

public service announcements (PSAs)   Free television or radio promotions of the programs and activities or services of government agencies, nonprofit organizations, and others that serve the interests of the community.[4]

publicity
Newsworthy information that, when released to the media, will be published or broadcast as news. It is used as free advertising.[7]

The use of selected media to carry messages and stories without cost.[4]

The dissemination of news and information concerning a person or organization through channels of communication such as newspapers, magazines, television, and radio, the use of which is not paid for by the publicity seeker.[5]

publicity release   Information with news value distributed to the media for purposes of favorably influencing consumers.[2]

pub-set   An ad prepared by a publication when submitted as copy and layout.[2]

put to bed   To close an issue of a publication, after which [time] no additional material may be inserted.[4]

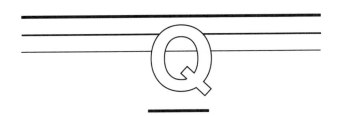

quiet enjoyment clause [A lease clause that] gives a tenant assurance that the landlord has authority to enter into a binding lease.[7]

radio A time   Monday through Friday, 6:30 P.M. to sign-off, and Saturday and Sunday all day.[2]

radio AA time   Monday through Friday, 9:00 A.M. to 4:30 P.M.[2]

radio AAA time   Monday through Friday, 6:00 A.M. to 8:00 A.M. and 4:30 P.M. to 6:30 P.M.[2]

radius [restriction] clause
A clause inserted into a shopping center retail lease establishing the distance from the center that the retailer may operate another, similar store.[7]

A specific trade radius in which a tenant may not operate another business, usually of the same type or name.[7]

rate card   A published list of advertising rates for any given medium.[2]

rate holder   The minimum-size ad that must appear during a given period if the advertiser is to secure a certain time or quantity discount.[2]

rates and data book   A publication that lists all pertinent information relating to newspapers published in the United States.[2]

rating
The estimated size of an audience expressed as a percentage of the specified universe.[4]

The percentage of a given universe who watch (listen to) a given station at a given time. A 10 rating means that 10% of the people universe (or household universe) were watching the show. Ratings can be added together. (*See* gross rating points.) However, since there is never a time when 100% of the homes have their TV sets turned on, ratings in a time period (quarter hour) never add up to 100.[5]

rating point   One percent of the homes in the measured area whose sets are tuned to a [specific] station: used for making comparisons of stations.[2]

raveling
The undoing of the texture of a pavement, typically through the loss of aggregate from the surface or the stripping of the asphalt cement from the aggregate; also called abrasion.[3]

A rough, pock-marked surface due to the undoing of the pavement through loss of aggregate from the surface or through stripping of the asphalt cement from the aggregate. The wheels of passing traffic break free pavement fragments.[14]

reach
The number of people who read, watch, or listen to a newspaper, magazine, television [program], or radio program.[4]

The total audience a medium actually covers.[2]

The estimated number of persons or households in the audience likely to be exposed to a commercial message at least one time in a designated time period.[4]

reach and frequency   Reach is a measure of the net percentage of homes (or viewers) reached by a schedule during a given period of time; frequency is the average number of times each home (or individual) that is reached saw that commercial. Reach and frequency are functions of the gross rating points of a schedule. (Reach × Frequency = Gross Rating Points.)[5]

real income   *See* income, real.

recapture   A right, usually held by major tenants, to deduct such items as common area maintenance or insurance paid from percentage rents that may be owing.[8]

recapture rate   The annual rate at which capital investment is returned to an investor over a specified period of time; the annual amount, apart from interest or return on interest (compound interest), that can be recaptured from an investment, divided by the original investment. Also called capital recovery rate.[7]

receipt of goods (ROG) terms   Cash discounts that begin when merchandise reaches the store.[5]

recoating   A procedure in both roof and parking lot maintenance in which a deteriorated surface is rejuvenated by a coat of, usually, a petroleum-based product.[7]

re-covering   The placing of a new roof over an

existing roof. This procedure may be done one time without the tearing-off of an existing roof membrane. Local codes will dictate reroofing policies.[7]

reflection crack
A crack pattern on the surface caused by cracking in the pavement underneath the surface, which is due to expansion and contraction.[3]

A surface cracks without a distinctive pattern that reproduces cracking of a similar pattern in the subsurface pavement layers. The undersurface cracks open owing to expansion and contraction.[14]

regional center
This center type provides general merchandise (a large percentage of which is apparel) and services in full depth and variety. Its main attractions are its anchors: traditional, mass merchant or discount department stores or fashion specialty stores. A typical regional center is usually enclosed, with an inward orientation of the stores connected by a common walkway, and parking surrounds the outside perimeter.[1]

regional tenant   A retailer who operates stores in a particular region of the country.[7]

relative draw analysis   A technique used to understand the demographic and geographic strengths and weaknesses in a center's draw.[4]

release   A manuscript sent to the media to announce information or convey a story.[4]

relocation clause   [A lease clause that] gives a

landlord the ability to move the tenant to another location within the shopping center
premises.[7]

renewal option An agreement at the time of
the original lease as to the terms of a tenant's
extension of lease term.[7]

rent/sales index A measure that helps determine whether a store's rent is in proportion to
the sales it generates. It is calculated by dividing
the percentage of rent by the percentage of
sales.[4]

rent-to-sales ratio A tenant's total occupancy
costs divided by its total sales, expressed as a
percentage. The ratio is an indicator of a tenant's financial viability.[4]

rental area
The square footage of a building that can actually be rented. (Halls, lobbies, elevator shafts,
maintenance rooms, and lavatories are excluded.)[5]

That part of gross floor area used exclusively
by individual tenants and on which rent can
be obtained.[6]

replacement In a strict sense, it implies remov-
ing some portion of the property and restoring
the missing part on a like-for-like basis.[13]

replacement cost Today's cost of construction,
without considering depreciation.[7]

replacement value The basis for loss payment
can, by endorsement (specifying changes in or
additions to the policy) and additional premium,

be changed from actual cash value (replacement cost less depreciation) to replacement value, which is the full cost of replacement as of that date. This change adds to the annual expense of insurance.[12]

reports Written documentation, based on investigation, describing events that took place during an incident.[7]

representative (rep) The salesperson or contact for any medium.[2]

reserve for replacement Monies put up by the owner or collected from tenants to be used for large repairs or replacements in the future.[8]

residual analysis An analytical procedure in which the potential for a store or a shopping center is derived on the basis of sales volume estimated to be available, based on population, income, and expenditure characteristics of the population, and allowing for the effects of present and future competing stores to obtain their operating sales volumes.[6]

retail The price at which goods are offered for sale.[7]

retail expenditures Spending for retail by trade area residents adjusted for income differences in relation to market universe retail sales, adjusted by the elasticity factor (= per capita retail expenditure). Projected into the future at a rate reflecting an increased standard of living (excluding inflation), generally 1.5% to 1.7% per annum simple. Multiplied by projected population, it yields total retail potential, i.e., expenditures incurred by trade area residents in existing stores, at home and elsewhere, and potentially in proposed facilities.[6]

retailer's cost price *See* net price.

retailing The business activities concerned with selling goods to ultimate consumers.[5]

retained earnings Accumulated income less distribution to stockholders and transfers to paid-in capital accounts.[3]

return on investment (ROI) analysis A formula used to determine the relative worth of an asset. There are many different kinds of analyses: they're usually used to determine if an asset should be repaired or replaced.[7]

reverse allowance The tenant pays a specific amount of money over any minimum and percentage rents for the landlord's cost of building the space.[7]

rider An amendment or addition to a document of record.[3]

right of subrogation Ordinarily, an insurance company that pays its insured for a loss has the right of action against a third party who may have been responsible for the loss. This right of action is called the right of subrogation.[12]

ripple A form of plastic movement at points where traffic stops and starts.[3]

risk The peril insured against; the chance of loss.[7]

risk management The branch of management

that is concerned with protecting a business against the risks of accidental loss.[7]

Risk Retention Act companies This 1986 federal act permitted industries to jointly set up insurance vehicles that were licensed in a single state and then to write business in other states.[7]

robbery Forcibly taking property directly from another person.[7]

ROG *See* receipt of goods (ROG) terms.

ROI *See* return on investment.

roof cement A cement normally used for minor repairs of a roof, such as nonrecurring leaks. It may be asphalt, a pitch-based plastic, or a flashing, and must be compatible with the original materials.[3]

roof deck The prepared subsurface of a roof on which a membrance is laid.[7]

roof repair The cost of routine maintenance and repairs to the roof of a center. It does not include the cost of major capital improvements.[10]

ROP *See* run of paper.

ROS *See* run of station.

run of paper (ROP) The placement of a newspaper ad in any portion as determined by the publication.[2]

run of placement (ROP) color In printing, this is a random placement of one or two colors in an ad, usually determined by the media representative.[4]

run of station (ROS)

Spot commercials bought for placement anywhere within a station's schedule (at its discretion). The ROS rate is generally the lowest offered by a station.[5]

Preemptible spot commercials bought for airing within a station's schedule, timed at the station's discretion.[2]

sales The amounts received by or accrued to the store in exchange for merchandise sold to customers during an accounting period.[4]

sales analysis report A report of actual sales and percentage of change over a given time. It also shows sales per square foot for each tenant or merchandise category.[4]

sales area Rentable area minus storage space. The proportion of rentable store area devoted to sales varies among store types and among stores of the same type, so that calculations of sales or rent are more uniform if made on the basis of total store area.[6]

sales benchmarks Allows comparisons of the center to other shopping centers in terms of sales, rent, and other statistics.[4]

sales contribution An estimate of how much of a center's sales come from a geographic or a demographic group. Sales contribution is a component of a center's share of market calculation.[4]

sales efficiency ratio A comparison, expressed as a ratio, of the percentage of a merchandise category's total square footage to its percentage of gross sales. The ratio is an indicator of category productivity.[4]

sales per square foot Total annual sales divided by the total number of square feet of rentable area.[6]

sales potential
Estimates of how much money the people who live in a market will spend on consumer goods and services.[4]

Total retail spending by trade area residents, usually stated in terms of store type. This potential is the product of the multiplication of population and per capita expenditures. The sales potential provides the support base for the planned new facilities as well as for existing competitive facilities both within and beyond the trade area.[6]

sales/rent report Information that helps evaluate the sales performance of a center and its stores. It is considered the center's "report card" and is an ongoing measure of productivity.[4]

sample size The determination of how many shoppers or market residents will be included in a shopper intercept or telephone survey.[4]

sans serif A typeface in which the letters have no serifs. *See* serifs.[4]

saturation A media pattern of wide coverage and high frequency during a concentrated time period, designed to achieve maximum impact, coverage, or both.[2]

scatter plan   The use of announcements over a variety of stations and time segments to reach as many people as possible in a market.[2]

screen halftones   Photographic illustrations in an ad whose image results from a percentage application of ink.[4]

scupper   A hole in a parapet wall of a roof that allows water to flow into the roof drain. A scupper also acts as an overflow precaution in case of a gutter blockage.[7]

sealers   Liquid coatings used to protect asphalt parking lots and roadways.[7]

search procedure   Step-by-step instruction on how to search an entire shopping center.[7]

seasonality index   A table of percentages of total annual sales generated at a shopping center during each selling season (holiday, winter clearance, spring, and so on).[4]

secondary market
The geographic market located outside the primary market from which a center obtains shoppers or sales. *See* also primary market; inflow market.[4]

A geographic term used to designate areas outside the primary market, the fringes of the market and beyond.[2]

secondary research   Information that has already been gathered by another party and is available. *See* primary research.[4]

secondary zone   The portion of a trade area that

supplies additional support to a shopping center beyond that obtained from the primary zone. Secondary zone patronage for a shopping center is primarily generated by the comparison shopping stores in the center; convenience shopping is primarily done by secondary zone residents at other neighborhood centers closer to home.[6]

secret shoppers A process by which individual stores are evaluated in terms of sales staff, merchandise techniques, store appearance, and other issues. Also called mystery shoppers.[4]

sector A smaller geographic division of a primary or secondary trade area. Sectors are based on geographic and demographic characteristics. They allow the trade area to be analyzed in greater detail.[6]

sector analysis Research into segments of a trade area to determine population, socioeconomic characteristics, rate of sales penetration, and sector market shares. Usually for focus advertising.[6]

security To the owner, security connotes the preservation of the buildings representing his investment and the maintenance of peace and order, the absence of which will deter shoppers. To the tenant, security revolves around protection of his merchandise and employees, plus that same interest in a peaceful environment for his customers. To the shopper, security has to do with personal safety and the safety of property while in the center or traveling to and from it.[12]

security chain of command The ordering of a security force by rank or importance.[7]

security expenses   This major category includes costs associated with security at the center. These include payroll and employee benefits of center-employed security personnel, the costs of contracted security services, equipment, uniforms, and supplies attributable to the security function.[10]

security revenue   Receipts from tenants to recover the cost of center security services.[10]

selectivity   In advertising, the ability to choose one medium or even one feature of a medium (ZIP code or family income) to suit an advertiser's needs.[4]

series discounts   A number of discounts offered by the manufacturer to the retailer.[7]

serifs   The short lines stemming from the end strokes of printed letters.[4]

share
Of all the homes that have their television sets turned on at a given moment, the percentage tuned to a given station. Shares for a given quarter hour add up to 100; rating points do not.[5]

A station's or program's portion of the total listening or viewing audience expressed as a percentage of the total [potential] audience.[4]

share of market.   An estimate of the percentage of a geographic market's sales potential that a center receives in sales.[4]

share-of-the-market analysis   An analytical technique in which it is assumed that strong stores, capably and aggressively merchandised, will obtain their representative share of the total market in that category, notwithstanding the existence of competing units. Stores that have an identifiable name appeal and impact on shopping habits, such as department stores, are strong enough to attract a certain share of total business under normal operating conditions.[6]

shopping center A group of retail and other commercial establishments that is planned, developed, owned, and managed as a single property. On-site parking is provided. The center's size and orientation are generally determined by the market characteristics of the trade area served by the center. The two main configurations of shopping centers are malls and open-air strip centers.[1]

shopper intercept survey
A tool used to gather information about a center's shoppers and shopping patterns.[4]

A survey conducted by stopping shoppers at the center.[4]

shopping goods Goods from variety, department, and general merchandise stores: toys, hobbies, sporting goods, small appliances, household, textile, garden and lawn supplies, luggage and leather, music, books, housewares, children's apparel, candy, radios, and televisions.[6]

shopping patterns Various types of behavior a consumer exhibits in a shopping center which are measured with consumer data tools. Shopping patterns might include the following: shopper origin, next destination, mode of transportation, primary purpose of center visit, shopping frequency, amount spent, time spent shopping, stores visited/purchased in, and buyer conversion.[4]

short rate   A print media term which means that the paper charges a higher rate if the advertiser does not fulfill its contract.[2]

shrinkage   The difference between merchandise on hand shown by a physical inventory and that shown as "book value." It may be due to theft, internal or external fraud, record distortion, waste, sabotage, general laxity, or careless operation.[5]

shrinkage cracks   Cracks usually having sharp corners or angles and identifiable by their tendency to run in any direction.[3]

sidewalk sale   A centerwide, merchants' association-sponsored, off-price, low-end promotion; merchandise is displayed from common areas fronting each store.[2]

sig cut   *See* logo.[2]

single-family house   A single detached structure of one unit.[6]

single ply   A type of roof made from a single layer of specially reinforced rubber or plastic.[7]

site   A specific tract of land proposed for center development, exhibiting qualities of size, shape, location plus accessibility, and zoning, and suited for the development of a center.[6]

slab The base on which roofing insulation is laid.[13]

sleepers Part of a bracing system that keeps HVAC [heating, ventilation and air-conditioning] units anchored and off the roof and limits vibrations to the premises.[7]

slip and fall litigation The type of lawsuit brought against a shopping center when a consumer is hurt by slipping on a defective surface.[7]

slippage cracks
Crescent-shaped cracks that usually appear in the direction of greatest traffic thrust because of a lack of bonding between the top layer of the pavement and the layer beneath. The top layer literally slips over the lower layer.[14]

Generally crescent-shaped cracks usually found in the direction where traffic thrust is greatest.[3]

slurry A type of asphalt sealer. There are different types, and usage depends on the kind of roadway and desired protection.[7]

small town rural A town outside of a U.S. metropolitan statistical area or outside of the suburbs of an urban core Canadian city.[10]

SMSA *See* standard metropolitan statistical area.

snipe A copy strip added over an outdoor poster or board containing special information.[2]

snow removal expenses The cost of snow removal from the building roof and parking lot and salting or sanding of the parking lot. It includes manpower, equipment, and material provided by an outside contractor or by the center.[10]

sodium light   A lamp in which light is produced by an electrical current passed through sodium vapor. Available in both high- and low-pressure applications.[7]

soft goods   Merchandise, also known as softlines, of nondurable character, such as wearing apparel, domestics (including linen, towels and bedding), and yard goods.[6]

space deadline   The lead time required by a publication to reserve advertising space for a specific date.[2]

special event   A centerwide, merchants' association-sponsored promotion aimed at generating increased customer traffic. [*See also* promotions or special events expenses][2]

special [marketing] assessment   A supplemental marketing contribution.[4]

specific performance clause   [In a lease, the clause that] gives one party the right to cause another party to comply with the lease.[7]

split run   A facility available in newspapers and periodicals whereby the advertiser alternates different advertising copy in every other copy of the same issue. This makes it possible to compare coupon returns from two different advertisements published under identical conditions.[5]

spot   A commercial announcement; also denotes schedules placed locally, as opposed to national network buys.[5]

spot color   An application of color to one or two places in an ad.[4]

staggered schedule   A schedule of space to be used in two or more periodicals, arranged so that the insertions alternate.[2]

standard inspection   A daily, weekly, or monthly examination of mechanical systems or other shopping center assets.[7]

standard metropolitan statistical area (SMSA)   A statistical unit defined by the Census Bureau as a county or a group of contiguous counties that contains at least one city of 50,000 inhabitants or more, or "twin cities" with a combined population of at least 50,000. In addition to the county or counties containing such a city or cities, contiguous counties are included in an SMSA if, according to certain criteria, they are socially and economically integrated with the central city. In the New England states, SMSAs consist of towns and cities instead of counties.[6]

standard operating procedure   A course of action that states precisely how a particular system of maintenance policy is to be conducted.[7]

standard operating procedures manual   A booklet that outlines a center's maintenance policy.[7]

step-down rents   Rents that are structured so that percentages paid on total sales by a tenant decrease as sales grow.[7]

step-up rents   Rents that are structured so that

they increase at specific times during the life of a lease.[7]

stock turnover
The degree of balance between a retailer's inventory and sales and the speed with which its merchandise moves into and out of a department or store.[7]

The number of times inventory turns over in a given period of time. It is calculated by dividing average inventory at retail into the net sales for the year. Average yearly inventory is the sum of the retail inventories at the end of each month added to the initial opening inventory and divided by 13, the number of inventories used.[5]

strip center
A strip center consists of an attached row of at least three retail stores, managed as a coherent retail entity, with on-site parking in front of the stores. GLA [gross leasable area] for the center must be at least 10,000 sq. ft. Open canopies may connect the storefronts, but a strip center does not have enclosed walkways or malls linking the stores. A strip center may be configured in a straight line, or have an "L" or "U" shape.[10]

A straight line of stores with parking in front and a service lane in the rear. The anchor store, commonly a supermarket in small strip centers, is placed either at one end or in the center of the strip. A strip center is usually a small neighborhood center, and the terms have come to be used interchangeably, although a strip may also be a large center.[12]

stun gun A small hand-held device that momentarily incapacitates an intruder through the use of an electrical current or charge. Illegal in many states.[7]

subcontractors [Sources of] skilled labor from specialized trades such as mechanical, electrical, fire protection, carpentry, painting, HVAC (heating, ventilation, and air-conditioning), and floor and ceiling fixtures.[11]

subgrade The prepared surface on which asphalt is laid.[7]

sublease
The renting or leasing of premises by a tenant to a third party, but with some portion or interest in them still being retained. Either all or part of the premises may be subleased, for either the whole term of the original lease or a portion of it. However, if the tenant relinquishes his or her entire interest, it is no longer considered a sublease but an assignment.[3]

The original tenant remains liable for the lease while a new tenant assumes occupancy.[7]

subordination clause Defines whether tenant or landlord obligations are recognized first in the case of foreclosure or sale of the property.[7]

subrogation The right of an insurance company to recover its loss from the responsible party after paying the policyholder's claim.[7]

substrate The base on which roofing insulation is laid.[13]

suburban center [A center] located in a less-dense city or town that surrounds either the central city of a U.S. metropolitan statistical area or the urban core of a Canadian city.[10]

suburban share   The portion of retail expenditures by the population in a trade area that is retained in stores outside of the downtown business district. The designation does not refer to political boundaries and is not meant to limit the term to those stores outside the city limits. The range of suburban shares for different retail categories varies from department stores, which register a substantial portion of their sales downtown, to food stores, in which nearly all sales are transacted in sections other than the central business district.[6]

superregional center
Similar to a regional center, but because of its larger size, a superregional center has more anchors, a deeper selection of merchandise, and draws from a larger population base. As with regional centers, the typical configuration is as an enclosed mall, frequently with multilevels.[1]

supervision fee   A fee added to common area costs to cover the owner's cost of supervising the contractors and bidding necessary work. Generally stated as a percentage of the actual costs.[8]

surety bonds
Payment and performance bonds usually used on significant construction jobs.[7]

Stand behind the general contractor's obligations to the owner under the terms and conditions of the contract. Generally such surety bonds cost ½% to 1% of the total contract amount.[11]

TAP *See* total audience plan.

TF *See* till forbid.

T-shaped center A center designed to accommodate three anchor stores, the T type has parking on all sides, with service provided through a tunnel or shielded service bays or a combination of both. T centers may be open or enclosed. Note that one anchor is not visible from the front entrances of the other two. Some authorities consider this a disadvantage in that shoppers may not be drawn to all parts of the center. Other authorities, however, consider this an advantage in that each anchor store provides an attraction helpful to the satellite stores in its vicinity.[12]

target audience
The consumers the advertiser wants to reach.[4]

The particular demographic group that [an advertiser] most wants to reach with advertising messages.[5]

tear sheet A printed, dated copy of an ad as it appeared; generally submitted with the invoice as proof of publication.[2]

tear-off   A roofing and asphalt procedure in which an old membrane or surface is removed as a prelude to replacement with a new product.[7]

teaser ads   Small ads, run in advance of a major effort, to arouse interest in a forthcoming campaign.[2]

telephone survey   A tool used to measure the competitive shopping patterns and perceptions among residents of a center's market area.[4]

tenant   A party who leases real property from the owner of the property (or of a leasehold interest in the property) for value considerations.[3]

tenant evaluation   A tool used to analyze the individual stores in a center in terms of their sales staff, variety and selection of merchandise, merchandising techniques, and store appearance.[4]

tenant improvements   Building improvements that enhance a tenant's space. May be paid for by either landlord or tenant.[8]

tenant mix
The distribution of store types within a retail complex.[4]

The types and price levels of retail and service businesses within a shopping center.[7]

tenant roster   The tenant roster is a master record. It lists such basic information as each tenant's name, the space number occupied, and the type of business being operated. It also lists key details in the tenants' leases, such as the square footage occupied, the rent per square foot and the total monthly rent, the lease date (which could be either the date it is prepared or the date it is signed), the commencement and expiration dates of the lease, and any special provisions.[9]

termination
1. Interruption of the lease before the term expires.[7]

2. The firing of an employee.[7]

tertiary zone   An outlying segment of the trade area that can be identified in certain circumstances as contributing a recognizable share of sales volume to a shopping center. This zone is designated when there appears to be a tributary area extending beyond the normal limits of the secondary zone, usually in a specific direction.[6]

theme/festival center   This center typically employs a unifying theme that is carried out by the individual shops in their architectural design and, to an extent, in their merchandise. The biggest appeal of this center is to tourists; it can be anchored by restaurants and entertainment facilities. The center is generally located in an urban area, tends to be adapted from an older, sometimes historic, building, and can be part of a mixed-use project.[1]

third-party insurance   [This insurance] protects the insured against liability arising out of property or bodily damage to others caused by another party.[7]

three-party agreement   A three-party agreement between the developer (owner), architect/

engineer, and general contractor is the traditional method of contracting. In this case, the
developer works closely with the architect/engi-
neer to plan and design the project. The developer explains the concept and the architect/
engineer executes the plans and specifications
accordingly. These plans and specifications are
then submitted to competing contractors who
estimate the cost and time it will take to complete the project.[11]

till forbid (TF)   An order to a station to run a
spot at the designated time until further notice,
or until the client orders them to stop.[5]

time value of money   The concept underlying
compound interest: that a dollar received today
is worth more than a dollar in the future, due to
opportunity cost, inflation, and certainty of
payment.[7]

tonnage   A measurement that determines the
strength of an HVAC [heating, ventilation and
air-conditioning] system. Also used as a determi-
nant to gauge air requirements for a tenant
space. One ton of air is equivalent to 12,000
BTUs [British thermal units].[7]

total audience plan (TAP)   A radio term for an
ROS run of station schedule. TAP Plans generally specify the number of commercials to be
aired in each daypart.[5]

total income   *See* income, total.

total personal income   *See* income, total personal.

total market coverage   A program offered by some newspapers that combines newspaper insertion with direct mail or direct delivery to saturate a geographic area.[4]

total rent   The minimum and percentage rent paid by a tenant, coupled with any extra charges that the tenant must pay.[7]

total survey area
A geographic area designated by rating services composed of all the counties in which approximately 98% of the area's home market station's viewing or listening occurs.[4]

The geographic area sampled in a rating survey. The total survey area is determined by the amount of viewing or listening done to stations in the market being measured. The total survey area of a market is larger and contains more counties than the ADI [area of dominant influence] of the metro area. Total survey areas are not mutually exclusive, as are ADIs.[5]

trade area
The geographic area from which a center draws its shoppers. Limits that define a trade area may be distance, natural barriers such as rivers, or man-made obstructions such as a highway that is difficult to cross.[7]

The geographic area from which the sustaining patronage for steady support of a shopping center is obtained. The extent of the trade area is governed in each instance by a number of factors, including the matter of the center itself, its accessibility, the extent of physical barriers, the location of competing facilities, and limitations of driving time and distance.[6]

The territory from which 85% to 90% of retail trade will come on a continuing basis.[12]

trade area zones   Those segments into which a trade area is normally divided in order to better illustrate variations in the probable impact of proposed shopping centers as regards distance, travel time, and competitive facilities. Most frequently, trade areas are divided into primary and secondary zones. In addition, a tertiary zone is sometimes indicated.[6]

trade discount   The manufacturer's or supplier's discount from the suggested list price; it is expressed as a percentage.[7]

trade fixture   An item specific to a tenant's business, usually not attached to the walls or floor; usually removed at lease expiration.[7]

trade name   The name under which a tenant operates a business.[7]

traffic   The number or volume of shoppers who visit a shopping center during a specified period of time.[7]

traffic estimates   Estimates based on counting the number of shoppers to understand how much traffic is in a center. This is also possible given a few items of research information: Divide the total annual center sales by the average expenditure per shopping visit to get the estimated annual shopping trips.[4]

traffic-building device   A center-sponsored promotional activity designed to stimulate customer traffic.[2]

transfer The sales volume transferred from the parent store or other branch units to a newly opened unit of the same store.[6]

triangle-shaped center Similar in many respects to the T-shaped center but with the added factor of providing visibility of all anchor stores from the front of each. A triangular design is likely to be somewhat wasteful of land, but it may be the optimum design for sites that are not rectangular. Designed to accommodate three anchors, the triangle center may have two levels, with parking around its perimeter. In most cases, when a center has two levels without a parking structure, it is designed with graded parking lots to allow entry at each level.[12]

triple net lease A lease in which 100% of all taxes, insurance, and maintenance associated with a shopping center is paid by the tenant.[7]

two-party design/construct agreement The developer works with a company that provides architectural/engineering *and* construction services. Under most state laws, a contractor cannot furnish these services unless he has *licensed* architects and engineers on staff.[11]

turn key The landlord builds and finishes out a retail space; the tenant shows up with merchandise and is ready for business.[7]

U-shaped center A strip center with two lines of stores placed at right angles to the strip, forming a U, with parking in front of the stores and service lanes behind them. U-shaped centers usually have more store space than L-shaped strips and consequently tend to be community-type rather than neighborhood-type centers. Because of their size, they may have as many as three anchors, one at each end and one in the middle, with the major anchor generally located in the middle.[12]

umbrella excess liability A form of insurance that protects against losses in excess of amounts covered by other liability insurance policies. It is used to protect against catastrophic losses.[7]

urban areas Incorporated localities with a population of 2,500 or more; residences of already settled suburban areas surrounding major cities. Population densities in excess of 1,500 persons per square mile.[6]

urban centers [Contributors] to the revitalization of downtown areas, urban centers are usually part of a city's urban-renewal program.

They usually include a pedestrian mall or covered walkways (particularly in areas of climate extremes) and are built right in the traditional shopping district. Characteristically, urban centers feature a parklike atmosphere, absence of cars, freedom to move about among a variety of retail stores, and, in many cases, a food court.[12]

use clause
A clause inserted into a shopping center retail lease that restricts the category of merchandise or items that a retailer is allowed to sell.[7]

An outline of the exact type of merchandise to be sold or business to be conducted in the premises.[7]

Tenants are restricted to providing the categories of merchandise or services specified in their leases and must obey any lease restrictions on how they operate.[9]

utilities expenses   This major category includes the cost of all utilities used in the common area of the center. It includes expenses for electricity, gas, and oil related to the common area, including exterior lighting. It does not include utilities purchased by the center and resold to individual tenants for consumption within their lease premises.[10]

utilities revenue   Any receipts from tenants for electrical or other utilities.[10]

V

vacancy rate   The square footage that is unoccupied, even if leases are signed and rents are being collected, expressed as a percentage of the total occupancy area of each store category.[10]

vandalism   Willful or malicious destruction or defacement of public or private property.[3]

vanilla box   A space partially completed by the landlord based on negotiations between tenant and landlord. Although every landlord's definition is different, a vanilla box normally means HVAC [heating, ventilation and air-conditioning], walls, floors, stockroom wall, basic electrical work, basic plumbing work, rear door, and storefront.[7]

variable expenses   Also called direct expenses; operating expenses that are affected by increases or decreases in sales volume.[7]

variance report   Usually part of the financial package provided to managers on a periodic basis. It shows the difference between budgeted expectations and actual results.[7]

vertical   A term used to relate a shopping center to a department store in urban areas.[2]

vertical-shaped center   A high-rise mall, which has escalators and elevators to carry people from floor to floor. Frequently the stores are placed around a central atrium. Such centers are usually in downtown areas or close to other high-density developments.[12]

video   The visual portion of a television broadcast.[2]

viewers per set (VPS)   The number of individuals in a demographic group viewing a particular spot, divided by the number of households reached by that same spot. VPS times homes equals audience expressed as persons.[5]

VPS   *See* viewers per set.

wait order An instruction by the advertiser to hold purchased schedules until instructed to proceed.[2]

waiver The surrender of a legal right.[7]

waiver of subrogation Each party to the lease gives up the right for its insurer to bring suit against the other party's insurer.[7]

warm brick Term for the unfinished space a tenant is given in a shopping center; the tenant is responsible for paying for all costs of store construction.[7]

warranty A statement that conditions will exist during the policy term and if found untrue, or not in existence, would invalidate the policy.[7]

welcome book Pamphlet given to tenants after signing a lease; it explains the ownership philosophy and introduces them to the center.[7]

white space Print media term referring to the blank space in an advertisement.[2]

workmen's compensation *See* workers' compensation.[7]

workers' compensation   A social insurance that entitles an employee to medical care and replacement of at least part of his or her wages if he or she is injured on the job. In return for this, the employee gives up the right to sue his or her employer. Claims are generally paid by private insurers, but the rates are set by state boards.[7]

zero-based budgeting A method of developing a current budget without basing it on any previous years' budgets; the starting point for each budget item is zero.[3]

ADDITIONAL SOURCES
OF TERMS

Following is a list of publications not published by the International Council of Shopping Centers (ICSC). This list may be used as a reference for additional terms and definitions that relate to the shopping center industry. The listing is not exhaustive and should only be considered as a sampling of potentially helpful sources with which to start further research.

ICSC does not recommend or endorse any products or vendors other than ICSC products.

The Dictionary of Real Estate Appraisal, 2nd Ed. Chicago, IL.: American Institute of Real Estate Appraisers, 1988.

Downes, John et al. *Dictionary of Finance and Investment Terms*. New York: Barron's, 1991.

Dumouchel, Robert J. *Dictionary of Development Terminology*. New York: McGraw-Hill Book Company, 1975.

Friedman, Jack P. et al. *Dictionary of Real Estate Terms, 2nd Ed.* New York: Barron's, 1987.

Harris, Cyril M. *Dictionary of Architecture and Construction*. New York: McGraw-Hill, Inc., 1975.

Hinkelman, Edward G. *Dictionary of International Trade*. San Rafael, CA.: World Trade Press, 1994.

Krieger, Murray. *The Complete Dictionary of Buying and Merchandising*. New York: National Retail Merchants Association, 1987.

Ostrow, Rona et al. *The Dictionary of Marketing*. New York: Fairchild Publications, 1988.

Ostrow, Rona et al. *The Dictionary of Retailing*. New York: Fairchild Publications, 1985.